Who do you say I am?

Who do you say I am?

*Lent and Easter Reflections
for a Holy City*

Joanne Woolway Grenfell
Adam Atkinson
Illustrations by Ali Mulroy

CANTERBURY
PRESS
Norwich

© Joanne Woolway Grenfell, Adam Atkinson 2024
Illustrations © Ali Mulroy 2024

First published in 2024 by the Canterbury Press Norwich
Editorial office
3rd Floor, Invicta House
110 Golden Lane
London EC1Y 0TG, UK

www.canterburypress.co.uk

Canterbury Press is an imprint of Hymns Ancient & Modern Ltd
(a registered charity)

Hymns Ancient & Modern® is a registered trademark of
Hymns Ancient & Modern Ltd
13A Hellesdon Park Road, Norwich,
Norfolk NR6 5DR, UK

Scripture quotations, unless otherwise indicated, are from New Revised
Standard Version Bible: Anglicized Edition, copyright © 1989, 1995
National Council of the Churches of Christ in the United States of
America. Used by permission. All rights reserved worldwide.

British Library Cataloguing in Publication data

A catalogue record for this book is available
from the British Library

ISBN 978-1-78622-569-6

Printed and bound by
Opolgraf Printing House

Contents

To enjoy the face of God, traced in every puddle of the city of people.

From The Beatitudes of the Bishop, used by Pope Francis in November 2021, quoting the writing of Archbishop Domenico Battaglia of Naples, and modelled on the eight Beatitudes given by Jesus in the Sermon on the Mount (Matthew 5.3–10).

Foreword

by the Most Revd Stephen Cottrell

This is the question that runs through this beautiful book. The question Jesus asked his friends then. The question he asks us now.

Through paintings and poetry, story and reflection, Joanne, Adam and Ali's words and pictures invite us to ponder and reflect ourselves. Who is Jesus? And what can his death and resurrection teach us today about who we are, how we treat one another and how we live our lives each day? The streets we walk, the food we eat, the places we go – none of this is untouched by Jesus' life and death and resurrection. It is woven into the story, so that this powerful retelling of what Easter means gives us the opportunity to reexamine Scripture in the light of who we are and to reassess who we are in the light of Scripture.

We are invited to rest awhile, turn our gaze onto a different landscape and see afresh what the Easter story looks like in this place and at this time. We are called to acknowledge the fragility of our lives and the vulnerability of our egos. Thus, we encounter on these pages not only the familiar stories of Scripture and the words of the liturgy, but also Shoreditch, Spitalfields and Stokey in London. We not only meet Jesus and Peter, but George Floyd, Sarah Everard and Child Q. The Easter story comes to life on our streets and in our lives. And Jesus asks again: 'Who do you say I am?' And who are you called to be as part of this story today?

+ Stephen Cottrell
Archbishop of York

Introduction

This is a series of meditations for Holy Week and into Easter. The meditations are based around readings for Palm Sunday, Maundy Thursday, Good Friday, Easter Sunday and the days beyond. The poems and prayers are by Adam Atkinson, the reflections by Joanne Woolway Grenfell, and the paintings by Ali Mulroy. We are colleagues who have a shared appreciation of ministry, poetry and art, who find that the spiritual landscape of our home city shapes our own identity as Christians.

Jesus asks the question of his disciples 'Who do you say I am?' in the Gospels of Matthew (16.13–16), Mark (8.27–29) and Luke (9.18–20). We have chosen to explore some answers to this question for our own time using readings from the Gospel of John.

The identity and personhood of Jesus and the responses they provoke in us run through all of the poems and reflections. Most of our passages contain the phrase 'I am', usually in relation to Jesus. Sometimes it is Jesus who defines who he is; sometimes it is others, for example, Pilate: 'Here is the man!' We also include the sharp questions asked of others about their identity and witness in relation to Jesus. For example, Peter is cornered into defining who he is not: 'You are not also one of this man's disciples, are you?' 'I am not.'

We began this work because of a conversation we had about prayer and writing. We wondered what the life, death and resurrection of Jesus would look like if lived out in the landscape of our home city. In the lives of our churches, we already enact the stories of our faith, bearing witness and carrying hope through the seasons of the year. The memory of Jesus is kept alive in school nativity plays, in carol services at Columbia Road flower market in Bethnal Green, in remembrance memorials in Bethnal Green Gardens, and in Trafalgar Square Passion plays. But we also wanted to reflect explicitly on the call to speak of Jesus in the social and political landscape of our city today and of other urban landscapes. Although we encounter many blessings and share many joyful celebrations, we also struggle to respond adequately to poverty, racism, loneliness and the myriad ways that society devalues and dehumanizes people – people who are made in God's image: each other, you and me.

The poems are all sonnets. In the creative space boundaried by this form's tight structure and undiluted expression, the poems present the person of Jesus through different actions and interactions, revealing conflicting perspectives, truths and identities. They imagine Jesus on the streets of his city and our city, the place where each of us lives and ministers. They contain themes that are especially relevant to us, and which might apply to any urban landscape.

The reflections offer imaginative responses both to the passages from John's Gospel and to the poems. They are intended to provoke readers both to reflect more deeply on the person of Jesus in the world today, and also to ask who they themselves are, as disciples. How does the person of Jesus change my identity, my past, my present, my future? In a quicksilver world where truth is contested, where modern-day Pilates laugh mockingly as they ask, 'What is truth?', we are invited to contemplate walking a path of integrity, courage and wisdom.

Both poems and reflections explore how the life, death and resurrection of Jesus Christ open for all of us a vision of dwelling simultaneously in the city of the present day and the city that is to come. The kingdom of God is not only to be found in the eternal city, but also in spaces and names with which we are familiar. For us, these are the streets of Shoreditch and Spitalfields, Stoke Newington and Shadwell. For others, it will be their own familiar landscapes, where life is lived and holiness encountered. And if these are the places *where* we are called to live, then *who* does Jesus say we are called to be in this time and in these places? Who do you say *I* am?

The Holy Saturday sonnets and reflections bring a brief pastoral interlude, where the Scriptures are almost silent. They focus on living with experiences of loss and grief. They give pause to ask, tenderly, what difference the cosmic moment of Jesus' death makes for ordinary lives lived and lost.

The Easter sonnets and reflections bring a joyful, celebratory note, with snatches of songs and rhythms of dance helping the gospel message to sing in our hearts and ring out across the city. They also bring a challenge: are we able to live our lives in a way that draws others into the love of God; are we able to share our faith in actions and words, so that others may know the Christ we share? For our church communities, there are hard questions too, prompted by Jesus himself. Are we even fishing on the right side of the boat, or are we simply repeating the familiar patterns of work and worship that may not help us to reach others today?

Ali's illustrations root all these reflections in real and imagined landscapes, giving colour and form to the people and communities who keep the rumour of God alive. They draw out difference and disagreement, truth and dissembling, through careful attention to light, dark and shade. Although points of detail draw us into the geography of the Gospel, Ali leaves space into which we can take some tentative imaginative steps and sketch out the contours of lives of discipleship in our own holy cities.

The three of us are aware, as we reflect and create, not only of the ways in which our responses come from the shape of our own lives as disciples, but also of the wider global and local context: the violence of international wars, the struggles of refugees in our city and country, and the realities of local violence are on our hearts as we minister in our own capital city. We are also aware of the numbers of faithful Christians, friends, strangers and exiles, from many traditions, cultures and backgrounds, who continue to seek Jesus as they live peacefully and hospitably in communities here and abroad.

We live in a world where freedom is contested. Not everyone can speak plainly and openly about the identity of Jesus or of how believing in him reveals the way to eternal life. At the same time, even in countries and cultures where faith can be practised freely, the habits of witness and proclamation are not easily passed on from generation to generation. Yet we know that we are formed as Christians by living out our faith on the streets of our cities and by breaking bread and telling stories around kitchen tables together. At the end of John 12, the disciples recognize that they have not understood all the signs that have been given to them. As they recollect together, they remember more and, as they continue to testify, the crowd around them becomes keen to hear of the signs of Jesus. It matters to our world who we say Jesus is.

Like those around Jesus, we may be reticent fully to own our identity as disciples. We may be unsure how to read the signs of Jesus for our age. We may notice that some gospel encounters take place in the half-light: we may even feel as if we are stuck waiting timorously with Peter around the charcoal fire outside the door of the high priest's courtyard. It may not only be Nicodemus who has initially to approach Jesus in the dark. Yet we will know that the story of God's love prevails for all of us; by Easter, even Nicodemus, even Peter, can walk in the light.

And with Jesus we will dance in that resurrection light.

So, let us follow Jesus through his death and passion, beyond the empty tomb, even to that Easter resurrection. Let us seek together who Jesus is calling us to be, as we ponder, who do you say I am?

Opening Prayer

Lenten Prose

Dear king, redeemer,
Seated on the throne,
My eyes are on you,
Jesus, full of tears.
Now please receive these,
My supplications.
You're the cornerstone;
The right hand of God;
Way of salvation;
Gate of heavenly life.
Make clean my soul from
All the dirt of sin.
Good Lord of glory,
I humbly beg you,
Lean down and listen
To this childlike cry.
Forgive us our debts,
Take pity, we ask.
We lay before you
The sins we repeat,
Choosing not to hide
Ourselves from your look.
With love, redeemer,
Speak absolution.
Innocent captive,

Who did not fight back,
Falsely accused and
Sentenced for sinners.
Save us, we pray you.
Lead us to echo
The answers of saints
To your question, dear
Jesus, 'Who do you
say I am?' Amen

I
Scene
Palm Sunday

Six days before the Passover Jesus came to Bethany, the home of Lazarus, whom he had raised from the dead. There they gave a dinner for him. Martha served, and Lazarus was one of those at the table with him. Mary took a pound of costly perfume made of pure nard, anointed Jesus' feet, and wiped them with her hair. The house was filled with the fragrance of the perfume. But Judas Iscariot, one of his disciples (the one who was about to betray him), said, 'Why was this perfume not sold for three hundred denarii and the money given to the poor?' (He said this not because he cared about the poor, but because he was a thief; he kept the common purse and used to steal what was put into it.) Jesus said, 'Leave her alone. She bought it so that she might keep it for the day of my burial. You always have the poor with you, but you do not always have me.' When the great crowd of the Jews learned that he was there, they came not only because of Jesus but also to see Lazarus, whom he had raised from the dead. So the chief priests planned to put Lazarus to death as well, since it was on account of him that many of the Jews were deserting and were believing in Jesus. The next day the great crowd that had come to the festival heard that Jesus was coming to Jerusalem. So they took branches of palm trees and went out to meet him, shouting, 'Hosanna! Blessed is the one who comes in the name of the Lord – the King of Israel!' Jesus found a young donkey and sat on it; as it is written: 'Do not be afraid, daughter of Zion. Look, your king is coming, sitting on a donkey's colt!' His disciples did not understand these things at first; but when Jesus was glorified, then they remembered that these things had been written of him and had been done to him. So the crowd that had been with him when he called Lazarus out of the tomb and raised him from the dead continued to testify. It was also because they heard that he had performed this sign that the crowd went to meet him.

(John 12.1–18)

Scene

Hypocrisy hangs thick in the city.
The streets stick fast with waste and vice and lust
As shops and tourists draining of pity
Ignore the broken man in veiled disgust.
Have-nots hang on, the queues snaking away.
Beneath arches of disregarded years,
Unjust power and pitiful week's pay
Here comes the broken man, becalming fears.
Newsrooms and politicians plan to save,
Initiatives are taken in our time.
The broken man seen staggering, who gave
And took on death in death, with love sublime.
The world's-played part is noise and violent facts.
The broken man with silent healing, acts.

Reflection

Earlier, in John chapter 11, Jesus is with Mary and Martha. Their brother Lazarus has been dead for four days. Martha and Mary admonish Jesus for not coming sooner. Jesus tells Martha that Lazarus will be raised from the dead. He also tells her who he is and what he will do. Lazarus is raised from the dead and walks, with his wounds still bound, from the tomb. Because of this and other signs of what Jesus is doing, the chief priests and Pharisees become even more wary of Jesus: they fear that others will start to believe in him because of his signs, and that the Romans will come and destroy their holy place and nation. In an act of worship and thanksgiving, Martha anoints Jesus' feet with costly perfume, and wipes them with her hair. Jesus' actions anger the chief priests, but they also draw further crowds, who gather with palm branches to make a way for Jesus to enter Jerusalem. People continue to testify, and the word spreads still further.

This is the setting for what Christians remember and re-enact as Palm Sunday, when Jesus enters Jerusalem. From here, the events unfold that lead to his last supper with his disciples, his death by crucifixion, and his resurrection on the day that we now call Easter. The beliefs that Christians hold, the witness that we bear, come back to this exchange between Jesus and Martha.

Jesus says, 'I am the resurrection and the life. Those who believe in me, even though they die, will live, and everyone who lives and believes in me will never die. Do you believe this?' Martha replies, 'Yes, Lord, I believe that you are the Messiah, the Son of God, the one coming into the world.'

Martha's response is a trusting affirmation of faith. The chief priests and Pharisees react with fear and wariness. Mary worships with love and adoration as she honours Jesus' body with her hands and hair. The crowds enact and amplify the authority of Jesus as they mark his physical path into Jerusalem, their shouts of 'Hosanna!' offering a plea for their city's deliverance. The Gospel writer joins the historical dots and connects Jesus' peaceful arrival, sitting on a donkey, with the Hebrew Scriptures (Zech. 9.9). The disciples do not at first understand, but later look back and begin to connect what Jesus did with what he said and who he was.

Each of these responses sets the scene for how we might bear witness, individually and collectively, to the person of Jesus.

We both discover and proclaim who Jesus is when we *affirm* our faith in him. This may take the form of a personal commitment to follow Jesus, voiced alone or to others; it will also be heard when Christians recite together the words of the creeds as part of their worship. An affirmation of faith need not mean that we understand everything fully or know every detail of why it matters, but it does mean that we have committed ourselves to seeking the truest and fullest understanding of who Jesus is, for ourselves and in community with other people of faith. It will also mean that we will keep on trying to unravel how we can assent to a universal declaration of faith by living it out in our own time and place.

When we *adore* Jesus in worship, we pour out our own love in response to what we see of God's love for us embodied in his son. For Mary, devotion is enacted through her body, with hands and hair. For us, adoration may mean sounds, sights, smells, tastes, gestures or posture as we bring together our inner intentions and our outer actions, in worship that glorifies God. We too can give thanks for the many gifts that he has given us, not least the presence of his son with us.

When we *acclaim* Jesus as our Saviour, we are doing more than sharing what we believe. We are praising and celebrating Jesus in a way that shares our hope and offers that hope to others. Even in the face of hostility or apathy, in good times and in bad, we can praise God freely, openly and generously. In East London, some of our local churches carry the body and blood of Jesus through the streets of Bethnal Green each year as part of their Corpus Christi celebrations – and their procession is met with smiling faces, loud honking car horns and cheers of support from people of many faiths and none. Acclamation does not need to be apologetic and need not be read as offensive if hope is paired with humility, the weakness and vulnerability of Jesus Christ as much in evidence as his power and majesty.

And then the work of interpretation follows. Making sense of who Jesus is needs us to connect and *apply* what we know of the stories of our faith to the stories of our lives today. Jesus' outpouring of sacrificial love joins us with the offerings and self-sacrifice of our Jewish ancestors but also with the possibilities of giving and sacrifice today, whether through voluntary acts, personal generosity, charitable giving or even just a cheerful response to the duties of taxation. Self-emptying can take many forms, but all of them start with our own consciences and hearts.

It matters who we say Jesus is. Belief has consequences. The chief priests plan to have Lazarus put to death, since it was on account of him that many were deserting and were believing in Jesus. There may be historical layers of witness and interpretation to peel back, but our own account of the life and hope that we know in Jesus is fundamental and needs to be passed on. The gospel continues to be good news for the world, but it will not be good news for anyone if it is simply preserved in a library of ancient accounts. It is a living truth, which needs witnesses to live and breathe and sing and dance it in their cities and their neighbourhoods.

Adam's poem, 'Scene', walks with us as we enter this city to reflect on the person of Jesus in our midst. It sets the scene for us to see broken people 'beneath arches of disregarded years' and to notice the lives that are written off as worthless. It takes us on a tour of 'shops and tourists draining of pity', showing how rampant consumerism reduces our humanity and makes us heartless. It points to the ways that employers, media and government grapple for profit and attention but fail to create space for all to thrive.

The poem also takes us to the broken man whom we recognize as Jesus himself, wounded and ultimately put to death by the world that he loved, staggering on our streets, meeting hate with love, and violence with peace. There's a stark contrast, underlined by rhyme, between the world's brutal noise and the silence of Jesus' loving, redemptive act on the cross: 'The world's-played part is noise and violent facts. / The broken man with silent healing, acts.'

Jesus not only brings healing and wholeness to our broken world but makes us refuse to settle for the pain and suffering that are caused by injustice. A love of Jesus brings with it a commitment to strive for God's kingdom of justice and peace, channelling our own efforts so that the light and life of Jesus' teachings can be known in all places, cultures and times.

With so much else going on – as we enter Jerusalem with Jesus, as we see afresh the streets of our own city, and as we look ahead to the heavenly city that God promises is waiting for us – we might feel that our own voices are inconsequential. But our witness matters. Martha's affirmation of Jesus – 'I believe that you are the Messiah, the Son of God, the one coming into the world' – sets off the chain of Holy Week events that take us to the cross and then to the empty tomb.

We too can tell the story of God's love: through the ways we act, through the music we make, through the songs we sing. Let us take Jesus' hand now and walk with him through our city's streets.

Prayer

Jesus, you are my
Dear king, redeemer,
Seated on the throne
Here I worship you.
My adoration
I pour out upon
Your feet and your head,
Soon to be pierced and
Crowned cruelly with thorns.
Move me on from fear
And from wariness.
I want these morning
Cries of 'Hosanna'
To stay on my lips
All through to nightfall.
May I worship you
Honestly, freely.
Please commission me,
And send me out with
Eyes to recognize
You in the broken.
May I be like you
Meeting hate with love,
Violence with peace.
I believe you are
The promised one who
Will restore all things.
Hosanna! Amen

2
Beautiful
Maundy Thursday 1

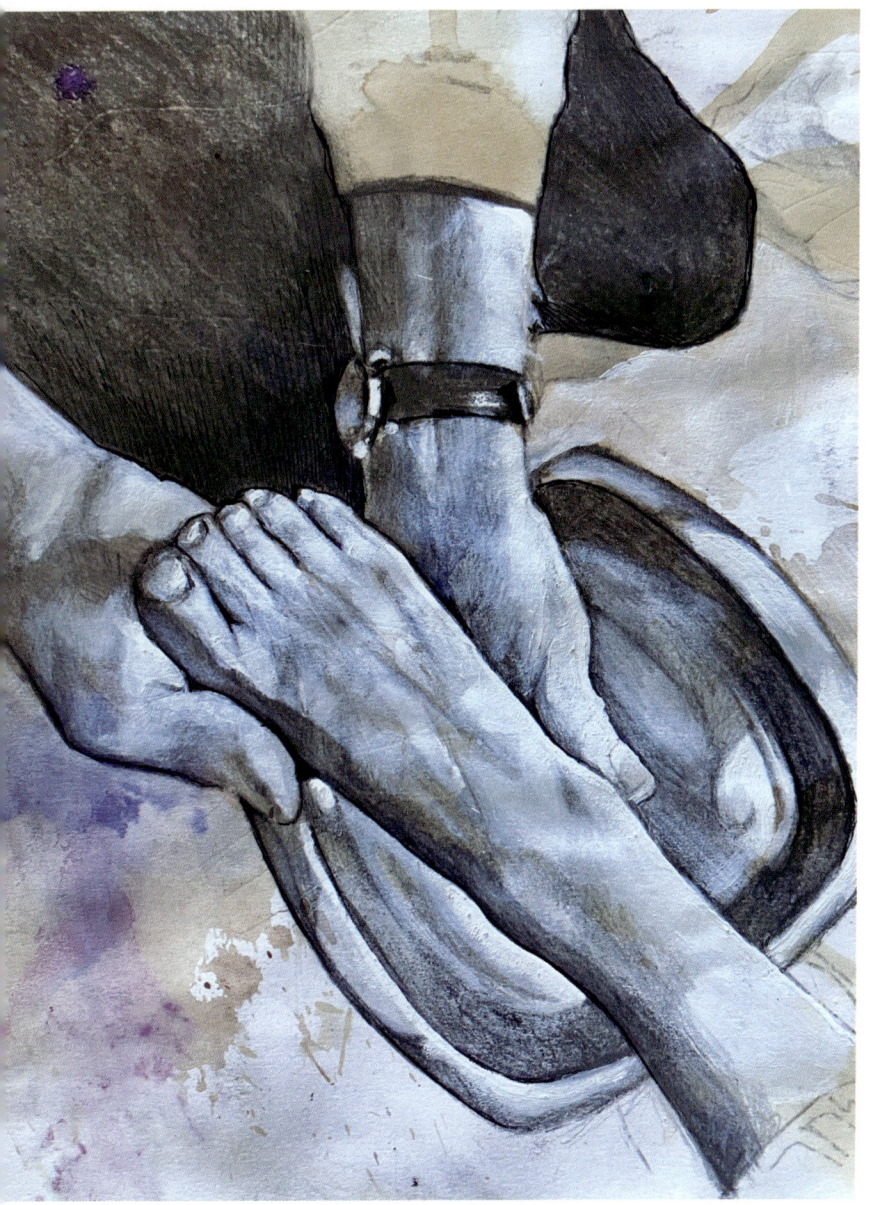

Now before the festival of the Passover, Jesus knew that his hour had come to depart from this world and go to the Father. Having loved his own who were in the world, he loved them to the end. The devil had already put it into the heart of Judas son of Simon Iscariot to betray him. And during supper Jesus, knowing that the Father had given all things into his hands, and that he had come from God and was going to God, got up from the table, took off his outer robe, and tied a towel around himself. Then he poured water into a basin and began to wash the disciples' feet and to wipe them with the towel that was tied around him. He came to Simon Peter, who said to him, 'Lord, are you going to wash my feet?' Jesus answered, 'You do not know now what I am doing, but later you will understand.' Peter said to him, 'You will never wash my feet.' Jesus answered, 'Unless I wash you, you have no share with me.' Simon Peter said to him, 'Lord, not my feet only but also my hands and my head!' Jesus said to him, 'One who has bathed does not need to wash, except for the feet, but is entirely clean. And you are clean, though not all of you.' For he knew who was to betray him; for this reason he said, 'Not all of you are clean.' After he had washed their feet, had put on his robe, and had returned to the table, he said to them, 'Do you know what I have done to you? You call me Teacher and Lord – and you are right, for that is what I am. So if I, your Lord and Teacher, have washed your feet, you also ought to wash one another's feet. For I have set you an example, that you also should do as I have done to you. Very truly, I tell you, servants are not greater than their master, nor are messengers greater than the one who sent them. If you know these things, you are blessed if you do them.

(John 13.1–17)

Beautiful

The hour was not at Cana. Water there
Was poured and given to the guests as wine.
This washing as a slave, he deigns to share
The loving as an act more than a sign.
He said the hour was coming at the Well,
The woman given water for her thirst.
This sating is a story we may tell
Again, of that the end is not the worst.
But now the hour is here. His robe aside,
With cleansing water, caring for my needs,
As preparation. Loving of his bride
In loving words and gifts and loving deeds.
Down, down the mountain runs the water sweet
To carry and to kiss beautiful feet.

Reflection

I wonder what it feels like to be Simon Peter and to ask Jesus as he begins to wash the feet of the disciples, 'Lord, are you going to wash my feet?'

There's so much going on in this time before the festival of the Passover. The disciples are used to Jesus being with them and eating with them. They've seen water turned into wine, people healed, crowds fed. They've even seen Jesus walking on water. Anything seems possible as the signs of a new creation emerge.

But now, as Jesus gets up from supper, takes off his outer robe, and ties a towel around himself, some further revelation is coming. As he pours water into a basin and begins to wash the disciples' feet and wipe them with the towel, there's an extraordinary moment of anticipation. A moment that's worth staying with because it leads us deep into questions of who Jesus is, how we experience him, and who we will be prepared to say he is.

'Lord,' says Simon Peter, 'are you going to wash my feet?'

Feet are tricky things, aren't they? I used to minister in a city cathedral which offered treatment for homeless clients by a podiatrist. When you are sleeping on the streets, feet are hard to care for; to keep dry and to protect from blisters and infection. And so, for feet to be tenderly looked after, nails trimmed, callouses softened, and dead skin removed, is a labour of love.

Even if we have homes and live comfortably, feet are still difficult. Baring them, having them cared for can feel uncomfortable, embarrassing and, well, … tickly! It's awkward to get our shoes and socks off, especially if we must balance on one leg and hop around, trying not to put a foot on a cold stone floor. Being the foot washer isn't easy either. Do we kneel, do we bend, how do we move from one person to the next? How do we manage the unexpected, ungainly intimacy that comes from sharing vulnerability?

'Lord,' says Simon Peter, 'are you going to wash my feet?'

I wonder where his emphasis lies. Are you going to *wash* my feet? Are you going to wash my *feet*? Are *you* going to wash *my* feet? So many questions – about the need for washing, about the nature of feet and the rest of his body, about the person of Jesus and how he acts, about Simon Peter's own unworthiness.

Simon Peter might not know exactly what is to come, who Jesus is, or where this story will end. But by now, as he watches other disciples have their feet washed, he surely has an inkling that Jesus is embodying something of God's new creation as he kneels at the feet of his people.

I cannot find words to describe the anticipation of that moment, but when I think of it I can feel a tingle in my spine and, yes, a tickle in my feet. Perhaps you can feel it too.

It is not just that Simon Peter is going to allow his feet to be washed, with all the helpless awkwardness of that moment. It is that by allowing – by wanting – his feet to be washed, Simon Peter is seeking intimacy with Jesus himself. He is saying yes at that moment to embarking on the adventure that is involved in daring to know ourselves as loved by our Creator. In vulnerable, human form, he is reaching towards God, who himself reaches through time and space to touch his beloved creation. And not just to touch, but to hold, to caress, and to kiss their feet.

There's an almost comical quality to Peter's reaction to Jesus, which briefly lightens the intimacy before Jesus drives his message home. Three responses, three movements.

First, the curious approach, asking for clarification: '*Are you going to wash my feet?*'

Second, a defiant retreat, setting a boundary: '*You will never wash my feet.*'

And third a glad assent, declaring that he is all in: '*Not my feet only.*'

When I look back on my own journey with God, I recognize these same three movements.

First, it has been necessary to acknowledge my own need: that I need God and that, through an overwhelming act of service that goes far beyond washing my feet, my Saviour can do this for me. That he has already done this for me.

Second, even as I have walked towards God, I have been likely at the same time to run away, to put up defences, to set a limit or a boundary on God's love. Not my feet. Not my need. Not my vulnerability. Not my sin. I deny my need of God even as I stand beside his Son and watch him wrap the towel around his waist ready to serve me.

And third, when my defences have eventually come crashing down, then I have wanted to fill myself full of the liberating, cleansing, healing love of God until I overflow. I have felt a longing so overwhelming for a love so abundant that I can't satisfy my desire for it, even as I acknowledge God in Jesus as my 'all in all' (1 Cor. 15.28).

This is a journey of faith.

Whether you are hearing for the first time Jesus' call to follow him, and to let him serve you; whether you are coming back, overcoming barriers to let Jesus draw you closer; or whether you are continuing to reach out in longing to become yet closer to Jesus: wherever you stand, barefoot and vulnerable, know that Jesus is standing right beside you. He has always been there, water and towel at the ready, waiting to touch and caress, and kiss your beautiful ugly feet. He loves you, and he will love you to the end.

Simon Peter's encounter with Jesus doesn't give him all the answers. 'You do not know now what I am doing,' Jesus says, 'but later you will understand.' For us too, understanding may be elusive, delayed, partial. It is only after their feet have been washed that Jesus reveals himself as Lord and Teacher to the disciples, 'for that is what I am'.

Who do you say I am? Lord, with power revealed through intimate vulnerability. Teacher, with signs pointing beyond himself to the knowledge of the Father.

Like Simon Peter, we may question, doubt and shut out Jesus many times. Like Judas, we may even turn away and betray Jesus. But Jesus still takes off his cloak, wraps a towel around his waist, and comes to us with abundant water to wash us clean. He comes to wash the whole world clean of sin, freeing us once and for all, accomplishing something through service and sacrifice and love that we could never do on our own.

In this moment of anticipation, we too can ask, with Simon Peter: 'Lord, are you going to wash my feet?'

Prayer

Dear God, as I pray
My eyes are on you,
Jesus, full of tears.
When you knew that your
Hour had come, you loved.
That same love you give
So freely to me.
You've always been there,
Ready to love me,
No matter how much
My words or actions
Refuse your kindness,
Willing to wash all
The dirt that I have
Accumulated.
So now, today, I
Acknowledge my need
Of you. Please save me.
I'm sorry when I
Try to put up a
Boundary against you.
I stand before you
Barefoot, vulnerable
And ask you to clean,
To heal, to fill me.
Thank you for your love,
That you will love me
to the end. Amen

3
Maundy
Maundy Thursday 2

'I am not speaking of all of you; I know whom I have chosen. But it is to fulfil the scripture, "The one who ate my bread has lifted his heel against me." I tell you this now, before it occurs, so that when it does occur, you may believe that I am he. Very truly, I tell you, whoever receives one whom I send receives me; and whoever receives me receives him who sent me.' After saying this Jesus was troubled in spirit, and declared, 'Very truly, I tell you, one of you will betray me.' The disciples looked at one another, uncertain of whom he was speaking. One of his disciples – the one whom Jesus loved – was reclining next to him; Simon Peter therefore motioned to him to ask Jesus of whom he was speaking. So while reclining next to Jesus, he asked him, 'Lord, who is it?' Jesus answered, 'It is the one to whom I give this piece of bread when I have dipped it in the dish.' So when he had dipped the piece of bread, he gave it to Judas son of Simon Iscariot. After he received the piece of bread, Satan entered into him. Jesus said to him, 'Do quickly what you are going to do.' Now no one at the table knew why he said this to him. Some thought that, because Judas had the common purse, Jesus was telling him, 'Buy what we need for the festival'; or, that he should give something to the poor. So, after receiving the piece of bread, he immediately went out. And it was night.

(John 13.18–30)

Maundy

On Shoreditch streets the sourdough outlets spill
To Spitalfields, with naan and cholla cob.
Up Stokey, shawarma spots are stuffed to fill
And even Shadwell's sliced white does the job.
East London's stuff of life begins the day,
It's lunch and tea, it's grub to keep and give.
In every season, setting, work and play
We feed, we need the broken loaf to live.
The simple table set, 'please sit' we're told.
And, starting with this meal, fresh, fragile, soft,
Begins a sequence. Helpless scenes unfold,
Another cut and tear. We look aloft:
Behold, 'I am' through whom all will be fed.
Into my hand is placed a piece of bread.

Reflection

There are two things that we all seem to agree on in interfaith gatherings in East London. The first is that we all stand together against racism, against the far right, and against anything that would disrupt the deep and warm friendships that exist between leaders and congregations in our diverse boroughs. 'Will you stand with us?' is the question that incoming new faith leaders are asked. 'Yes, I stand with you.'

The second is that we like to eat together. And not just polite nibbles at the back of church, Anglican style, but iftar tables groaning with wraps and rolls and rotis, Eid baklava delivered unexpectedly to the vicarage front door.

Adam's poem reminds me that we call bread by many different names: naan, pide, pitta, challah, sourdough, Mother's Pride. But whoever is hosting, and whatever it is called, we like to eat it, and we like to eat it together.

'We feed, we need the broken loaf to live', in the words of the poem, with an elegant internal rhyme, feed / need. Of course, it's different for many of our neighbours, but bread is my daily reminder of the one, Jesus Christ, in whom all our hungers are satisfied. I need. I feed.

When Jesus and his disciples sat together to eat, they would have remembered the Scriptures foretold that the Messiah would be betrayed by someone close to him. Jesus wants his disciples to know that he is the Son of God, and to believe 'that I am he'. He warns them of what is to come before the betrayal happens, confiding in Simon Peter that it will be 'the one to whom I give this piece of bread'. And then he dips it and hands it to Judas, son of Simon Iscariot.

The Scriptures aren't immune from 'othering' or scapegoating different communities, and John's Gospel needs careful reading to separate out the blame of individuals and authorities from the demonizing of whole cultures and peoples. At this point, we would be wise to notice that the betrayal of Jesus, from which the events around the crucifixion and death of Jesus develop, starts from someone who is very close to him.

As we watch the disciples gathered around Jesus for this Last Supper, we witness the heartbreak that comes when trust is abused by someone within our family or household of faith. We may be carrying with us our own experiences of abuse and betrayal and the moral injury that is caused when we are hurt by those from whom we ought to be able to expect better. We might also be aware, if we hold positions of power, that we may have betrayed the trust of others and caused them injury. Although many expect threats to come from those who are different from us and those beyond the boundaries of our own community, the truth is that the greatest harm often comes from those close by or within.

For churches, there is a reckoning to be had that we have not kept people safe from harm within our walls. Some in authority have abused children and adults, even as they have led, taught and broken bread on behalf of Christ's disciples today. They have left individuals with burdens of hurt and shame, and have broken the wider bonds of friendship in communities for whom they have been given the cure of souls. As bread has been broken and shared, bodies, hearts and souls also have been broken and abused.

Adam's poem conveys the local and particular beginnings in the Gospel accounts of Jesus' inevitable and far-reaching betrayal: 'And, starting with this meal, fresh, fragile, soft, / Begins a sequence. Helpless scenes unfold, / Another cut and tear.'

It is not only bread that is cut and torn when abuse takes place, but also consciences, bodies and souls. Damage may be lifelong, caused not only by an abuser, but by institutional obfuscation and cover-up. The warmth and light of a shared meal may feel forever out of reach for those whose whole being has been abused, and whose trust has been betrayed.

Judas' betrayal is almost lost in the hubbub of the shared meal, hidden in plain sight as Jesus answers Simon Peter's question: 'Lord, who is it?' 'It is the one to whom I give this piece of bread when I have dipped it in the dish.' We never hear from Judas, never know who he would say Jesus is, never understand his motivations.

Judas has seen others witnessing to the person of Jesus: Mary who anoints him with costly perfume, John who leans in and stays close, even Simon Peter, who gets it so badly wrong but who then experiences sorrow after his own denial. Judas cannot do the same. He is offered bread, and he receives it, but we never hear that he ate it. I wonder if he perceives that it is spiritual food and knows himself to be judged by the generosity of its gift. Whatever the reason, his response is to slip out into the night, putting himself into darkness.

This gap in the narrative may give us the opportunity to bring to the surface and to read our own intentions into Judas' actions. When have I betrayed my Lord? Insofar as I have had power, when have I abused that power? When have I distorted even prayer or worship because of the murkiness of my motivations?

No one is cast out from the community that gathers around Jesus to eat, but sometimes the sharp, searching light of communion and community will be too much for us to bear. Instead of walking towards the light, we may find ourselves choosing to slip out into the dark of night.

Even on the edge of such a moment, grace can still find us, and fresh bread can be pressed into our hands *for us to eat*. Even as we fear judgement, grace opens our imagination to the possibility of repentance and redress. *Take, eat.*

The death and crucifixion that follow for Jesus after Judas' betrayal are precipitated by his action, but they are still chosen willingly by Jesus, who died that we might be reconciled to God. Whatever we have done, the love of God is not defeated by sin. The darkness does not overcome it. We can open the door again, and step back into the light.

Prayer

Dear Jesus, I ask,
Please listen to these
My supplications.
Allow me to know
Your grace. Your free gift.
Open my senses
Again to receive.
Truly satisfy
The hunger in me.
Satiate all these
Distorted instincts,
Healing and mending
Them in the process.
May I find flavour
In you that nothing
And nobody can
Possibly give me.
Nourishment that is
All-sufficient, give
To those I love, and
To the world, and may
All who lack be fed.
I relish all the
Purity and the
Holiness you are.
May this very seed
Be pressed into my
Heart, I ask. Amen

4
Taken

Good Friday 1

After Jesus had spoken these words, he went out with his disciples across the Kidron valley to a place where there was a garden, which he and his disciples entered. Now Judas, who betrayed him, also knew the place, because Jesus often met there with his disciples. So Judas brought a detachment of soldiers together with police from the chief priests and the Pharisees, and they came there with lanterns and torches and weapons. Then Jesus, knowing all that was to happen to him, came forward and asked them, 'For whom are you looking?' They answered, 'Jesus of Nazareth.' Jesus replied, 'I am he.' Judas, who betrayed him, was standing with them. When Jesus said to them, 'I am he', they stepped back and fell to the ground. Again he asked them, 'For whom are you looking?' And they said, 'Jesus of Nazareth.' Jesus answered, 'I told you that I am he. So if you are looking for me, let these men go.' This was to fulfil the word that he had spoken, 'I did not lose a single one of those whom you gave me.' Then Simon Peter, who had a sword, drew it, struck the high priest's slave, and cut off his right ear. The slave's name was Malchus. Jesus said to Peter, 'Put your sword back into its sheath. Am I not to drink the cup that the Father has given me?' So the soldiers, their officer and the Jewish police arrested Jesus and bound him. First they took him to Annas, who was the father-in-law of Caiaphas, the high priest that year. Caiaphas was the one who had advised the Jews that it was better to have one person die for the people.

(John 18.1–14)

Taken

A dread-dark garden. Judas came to take,
With cops and squaddies, for a body snatch.
It's stop and search, snide stepping in with fake
Forgetfulness, 'Oh you, well what a catch!'
A sharp blade thrust in panic and in fear.
The boys won't win but, spoiling for a fight,
Are stopped as Malchus reaches for his ear –
And off they scarper back into the night.
So lifting up the cup of sorrow, pain,
To swallow all the poison antidote,
Hold healing to my head, turn loss to gain
He goes, as to the slaughter of a goat.
The one who walks this night says 'I am he.'
Look, leading through to day. 'You follow me.'

Reflection

If a detachment of soldiers, a squad of police or a delegation of religious leaders came looking for me, with lanterns and torches and weapons, I'd find it very hard to step forward into the light and say who I am.

As a woman, I'd feel my physical vulnerability, even – maybe especially – if an officer showed me his ID card. If I were young or Black or poor, I might fear being falsely accused of some criminal act. George Floyd, Sarah Everard and Child Q all discovered that even in supposedly benevolent states, the forces of law and order can exercise their power in ways that are unlawful and disordered. Sometimes it is not clear who belongs to the light and who belongs to the dark; trust may be manipulated, and appearances played in ways that make some more vulnerable than society would have us believe.

In faith communities too, power is abused as truth is weaponized. Interrogation in the name of orthodoxy comes straight from the playbook of oppression. And if I fear I belong to the wrong religious tribe, I may wonder if my answers are correct or acceptable, to those who use distortions of light as power and might.

But the Jesus of John's Gospel does not hide from the search. Instead, he steps forward and provokes an interaction. He makes the officers define whom they are seeking. And then he is clear: 'I am he.'

And the result is that he is arrested, 'Taken', in the title of Adam's poem. Confronted, bound and taken.

In tense encounters on our city streets, aggression is cheap. Gang member to gang member, youth to police, police to youth; mistrust builds mistrust and violence breeds violence. In the poem's tight alternative line rhymes, 'A sharp blade thrust in panic and in fear' leads swiftly to the cutting off of Malchus' ear; an almost casual injury, born out of Simon Peter's misplaced loyalty. Like many panicked, fearful acts, it is catastrophic because it escalates the violence.

And violence radiates outwards beyond capital cities, catching the young and impotent in the wide orbit of county lines, cuckooing vulnerable adults to create bases for drug distribution, building networks of crime on stolen identities, lives and futures.

There's a sharp contrast in 'Taken' between the officer's false persona and the clarity of Jesus' identity when he steps forward. 'It's stop and search, snide stepping in with fake / Forgetfulness, "Oh you, well what a catch!"' The use of 'snide' trips us up because we are expecting the more familiar '*side* stepping' to capture the threatening jostling of the encounter. But 'snide' is on point. We present false selves when we have no clear sense of our own core being, no grammar of love to inform our decisions or shape our lives. We assume the worst of others too, expecting that our puffed-up egos will meet only their angry fragility. We choose to mock when we do not dare to love. We reach for weapons when we don't know how to embrace.

And in this cut and thrust moment, as the poem turns into its final set of six lines, Jesus peaceably stands, fully himself, ready to lift the cup of sorrow and end the cycle of aggression. Everyone knows that the usual outcome is for there to be no victory: 'The boys won't win.' But Jesus chooses not to force a victory, and instead ends the violence through love.

It's usually poison that has an antidote, not violence, but the poem's metaphor of Jesus 'lifting up the cup of sorrow, pain, / To swallow all the poison antidote' is apt when we understand how violence poisons relationships, taints trust and contaminates communities. Showing Jesus choosing to sacrifice himself for others to go free, John demonstrates that violence has an antidote. God's power is relinquished to heal the world with love.

'For whom are you looking?' 'Jesus of Nazareth.' 'I am he.' Three times, the Gospel repeats Jesus' affirmation. Jesus is clear who he is and where this encounter is leading, as he asks, 'Am I not to drink the cup that the Father has given me?' Although this is just the beginning of the longest of nights in this 'dread-dark' garden, the poem brings us hints of the light that will break when the identity of Jesus will dawn upon the world: 'The one who walks this night says, "I am he." / Look, leading through to day. "You follow me."'

The rhyme of the final two lines cements our connection between the identity of Jesus, who he is, with our call to follow him. It is no longer a matter only of who Jesus is, but of who we will say he is, and who we will be in response. God invites each of us to follow Jesus through his passion and death, becoming part of the story of his love, and shaping our lives through his light and peace.

Who do you say I am?

Prayer

Dear Jesus, I know
You're the cornerstone,
The right hand of God.
Unshakeable rock,
With such clarity
Of who you are and
Where this is going.
I look to you for
Fresh direction, for
Boldness, courage, for
Certainty beneath
My feet, to speak and
Think and act for thee.
Thank you for going
In my place. You have
Stepped forward to take
The path of pain so
I am released, free.
My daily life, the
Future for my friends,
My neighbours is so
Unknown. My fragile
Soul needs a solid
Base. And there you stand,
Light. Not overcome.
You, around whom the
House of my life is
Being built. Amen

5
Skulking
Good Friday 2

Simon Peter and another disciple followed Jesus. Since that disciple was known to the high priest, he went with Jesus into the courtyard of the high priest, but Peter was standing outside at the gate. So the other disciple, who was known to the high priest, went out, spoke to the woman who guarded the gate, and brought Peter in. The woman said to Peter, 'You are not also one of this man's disciples, are you?' He said, 'I am not.' Now the slaves and the police had made a charcoal fire because it was cold, and they were standing round it and warming themselves. Peter also was standing with them and warming himself. Then the high priest questioned Jesus about his disciples and about his teaching. Jesus answered, 'I have spoken openly to the world; I have always taught in synagogues and in the temple, where all the Jews come together. I have said nothing in secret. Why do you ask me? Ask those who heard what I said to them; they know what I said.' When he had said this, one of the police standing nearby struck Jesus on the face, saying, 'Is that how you answer the high priest?' Jesus answered, 'If I have spoken wrongly, testify to the wrong. But if I have spoken rightly, why do you strike me?' Then Annas sent him bound to Caiaphas the high priest. Now Simon Peter was standing and warming himself. They asked him, 'You are not also one of his disciples, are you?' He denied it and said, 'I am not.' One of the slaves of the high priest, a relative of the man whose ear Peter had cut off, asked, 'Did I not see you in the garden with him?' Again Peter denied it, and at that moment the cock crowed.

(John 18.15–27)

Skulking

With Peter, the one loved by Jesus walks
Into the half light, a disciple still
But skulking. Soon the Galilean talks,
The questions burn his face against the chill.
Allegiance, friendship, what is right and wrong.
Decisions, consequences – getting hot?
Do tell, we want to know if you belong
In him. Protection blurts out 'I am not!'
Not what? Not kind or made of much full force.
Unbridled instincts, ego run amuck,
Not much of a disciple. Then, of course,
The shadows hide my shame as he is struck.
Imagining these scores against me filed,
He turns and looks, and loves, and calls me 'child'.

Reflection

Even when Peter is brought in through the gate by the other disciple, he is left outside in the courtyard.

We might know how it feels to be fearful and left out. Our ego crumbles and we look for ways to bolster it. We jostle and laugh our way into a group – any group – with the aim of being accepted. Feeling excluded, we exclude others in return.

And so, Peter warms himself at the charcoal fire with the slaves and the police. Like others congregated around braziers of belonging – soldiers, strikers, protesters, the homeless – he seeks what community he can find, pursuing light and meaning by gathering with others.

Sometimes gathering brings the light and warmth of solace and solidarity. Sometimes it keeps us in the shadows. In Adam's poem, it leaves us in the half-light, disciples still, but skulking. Keeping clear of the dangers of light and open space, we are left in murk, our fragile identities reinforced by the thinking of others: selves subsumed in affinity, truth shrouded in darkness. Skulking.

Group belonging leads here to groupthink. 'You are not also one of this man's disciples, are you?' the woman guarding the gate asks, the negative phrasing of her question offering Peter a cheap way out before he has even had time to ask himself, who do I say Jesus is?

I live in a world and a culture where I can speak plainly and openly of Jesus. I do not need to seek out others to strengthen shaky or hidden beliefs. I can call Jesus my Lord and my God. I can seek through him the way to eternal life, and I can share this way with others. I can make decisions, use money, hold power, in ways that honour what he has taught me.

But do I? How shy, how reticent, how awkwardly English am I when pressed to proclaim his death and resurrection. How fickle, how flighty, how flickering are my decisions and my resolve when I try to live his way – in my family, in my church, in the worlds that I so confidently inhabit. How unwilling am I to examine my conscience and bridle my power, giving it away to the vulnerable and the powerless.

I shun the light. I skulk.

What is it that I fear? Jesus, who is soon to pay such a hefty price for being the Son of God, does not seem to fear anything. He is clear who he is. 'I have spoken openly to the world ... I have said nothing in secret.' Jesus affirms this, also three times. 'I am.' 'I am.' 'I am' (John 18. 5, 6, 7).

The light and truth of Jesus expose the failings of those around him, and of all of us. In the poem, we see the high priest's questions burning Jesus' face against the chill – they are searching, searing, painful, as truth demands.

'Getting hot?' And then they turn their searchlight on Peter, 'Do tell, we want to know if you belong / In him', the poem's soldiers mock. Who do you say I am? Who do you say you are? Do you belong in him? And Peter denies it, three times. 'I am not.' 'I am not.' 'I am not.'

There is so much more to say on being in him, in Christ, understanding how our identity, our belonging and our behaviour come in focus when we encounter the Son of God. But for now, we stand with Peter, in the courtyard's half-light, unsure how to define ourselves or to defend our friend Jesus. Who seems unable to be strong. Who allows his face to be struck. Who looks to save others, not himself.

A strong Jesus, we could get behind. We could hide under the shadow of those wings. Gathered around charcoal fires the world over we could find new groups with which to agree, new shade in which to hide, new allegiances and dependencies to arm both bodies and minds, hopeful that we will be on the side of might when all is done and dusted.

But this Jesus, who do we say he is? We don't know who he is when he refuses to show his power, and instead steps calmly into the light and the truth. Jesus does not fear being alone, but we do, and so we huddle nearer the charcoal fire, retreating into half-light as the action gets physical. In the poem's words, 'Then, of course, / The shadows hide my shame as he is struck.'

I can't imagine Peter's moment of self-revelation as the cock crows, also three times, and the betrayal that was foretold is now announced. But I can imagine my own. *Not much of a disciple.*

Jesus never abandons us to the half-light of a charcoal fire but brings us into all truth and all light. Jesus never counts the cost of our betrayal, but cancels our debt, bringing us to newness of life, without guilt or shame. Jesus leaves no one alone in the courtyard. Jesus leaves no one outside the gates of love.

Whatever our fears, faults or failings, Jesus offers each of us salvation. With a look of love, he seeks us out and draws us close. In the final words of the poem, 'Imagining these scores against me filed, / He turns and looks, and loves, and calls me "child".'

Who do you say I am?

Prayer

Jesus, you are the
Way of salvation,
Gate of heavenly life.
Help me when tempted
To hide in shadows,
To think like the group,
To remain silent
When asked about you.
Thank you for taking
My place in the heat
Of the ultimate
Interrogation.
I'm so grateful that
You answer for all
My shame and my guilt.
You never leave me
But, walking with me,
Draw me to the kind
Light of your great love.
Purify my lips
In speaking for you.
Strengthen my resolve
In living for you.
Help me to follow
In your way of life
That's everlasting.
I worship and I
Adore you. Amen

6
Sentences
Good Friday 3

Then they took Jesus from Caiaphas to Pilate's headquarters. It was early in the morning. They themselves did not enter the headquarters, so as to avoid ritual defilement and to be able to eat the Passover. So Pilate went out to them and said, 'What accusation do you bring against this man?' They answered, 'If this man were not a criminal, we would not have handed him over to you.' Pilate said to them, 'Take him yourselves and judge him according to your law.' The Jews replied, 'We are not permitted to put anyone to death.' (This was to fulfil what Jesus had said when he indicated the kind of death he was to die.) Then Pilate entered the headquarters again, summoned Jesus, and asked him, 'Are you the King of the Jews?' Jesus answered, 'Do you ask this on your own, or did others tell you about me?' Pilate replied, 'I am not a Jew, am I? Your own nation and the chief priests have handed you over to me. What have you done?' Jesus answered, 'My kingdom is not from this world. If my kingdom were from this world, my followers would be fighting to keep me from being handed over to the Jews. But as it is, my kingdom is not from here.' Pilate asked him, 'So you are a king?' Jesus answered, 'You say that I am a king. For this I was born, and for this I came into the world, to testify to the truth. Everyone who belongs to the truth listens to my voice.' Pilate asked him, 'What is truth?' After he had said this, he went out to the Jews again and told them, 'I find no case against him. But you have a custom that I release someone for you at the Passover. Do you want me to release for you the King of the Jews?' They shouted in reply, 'Not this man, but Barabbas!' Now Barabbas was a bandit

(John 18.28–40)

Sentences

You say I am a king and you are right
Enough to start a dialogue, to ask,
But listen to the truth: You've picked up lies
About me off the way. Not that type king.
My kingdom is no empire ruled by might.
The world is not my reference nor my task.
I am beyond all that you think as wise,
I've granted all the benefits you bring.

What accusation brings us to this fight?
I find no case, no crime to now unmask.
I do not understand why someone dies.
Religious rules are always troubling.

You are our Lord, not Him. Release instead
A killer and the cost fall on our head.

Reflection

Sometimes, words roll off the tongue. And in Adam's poem, 'Sentences', they do just that, cascading from line to line, falling off cliffs on to ledges below: 'You say I am a king and you are right / Enough to start a dialogue, to ask.' Meaning is left hanging; myriad possibilities remain unspoken.

We tumble through the rhymes of the first twelve lines. Even if we only read the last word of each, we'd still get a sense of the drama of Jesus and Pilate's encounter: right, ask, lies, king; might, task, wise, bring; fight, unmask, dies, troubling. Can you feel the movement, can you hear the pattern?

Amid so many words, truth is hard to find. Pilate's words are in danger of defining who Jesus is: 'You say I am a king.' But the Jesus of John's Gospel is clear that his identity will not be given to him by the world's words but comes instead from the one who sent him.

Jesus will not be pigeonholed as a political leader, a revolutionary, a usurper of Pilate's authority – though who he is will have profound implications for all empires and dominions. Jesus will not stir up his followers to fight against being given up to those with whom he disagrees: 'If my kingdom were from this world, my followers would be fighting to keep me from being handed over.'

'Be there, will be wild,' Donald Trump encouraged his supporters, and in January 2021 the people surged up Capitol Hill.

Nor will he play games with words. There are no Humpty Dumpty moments with Jesus. 'When I use a word,' said Humpty in *Through the Looking Glass*, 'it means just what I choose it to mean – neither more nor less' (Lewis Carroll, 1871, ch. 6). Jesus defines himself differently: neither a word among many, vying to be heard in the clamour, nor an empty vessel of meaning, shape shifting until he finds audience approval. Instead, he is the Word – the Word who is God incarnate, the Way, the Truth and the Life.

'For this I was born,' Jesus says, 'and for this I came into the world, to testify to the truth. Everyone who belongs to the truth listens to my voice.'

Listening for the voice of Jesus, learning the grammar of love, seeking out the way of truth leads us into fullness of life. This is hard when modern-day Pilates ask, 'What is truth?' To listen demands a reshaping of the sentences of our lives and a reordering of them with integrity, courage and wisdom. It means saying what is unpopular, amplifying those whose stories are manoeuvred to the margins, seeking the longer, deeper view which distils virtue from an abundance of perspectives.

What is the alternative to listening for his voice? Pilate does not really have an answer. Adam's poem captures the meaninglessness of Pilate's platitudes. 'Religious rules are always troubling.' Indeed.

How can this sentence end? What sentence shall be handed down?

However many times we read Pilate's decision to release Barabbas and to crucify Jesus, we still hope that it will be Jesus who will be saved. And we long for this despite the irony that we ourselves are well capable of being participants or bystanders in a crowd that is baying for the sacrifice to be Jesus.

The poem's first eight lines belong to Jesus, the next four to Pilate. It becomes clear as we read that the last two lines, a rhyming couplet, are the voice of that baying crowd. They bring both a neatness and an ugliness to the sentence – though the story is, as we know, still far from complete. The capital letter of 'Him' reveals the crowd's judgement and the story's familiar betrayal: 'You are our Lord, not Him. Release instead / A killer and the cost fall on our head.'

Pilate is their Lord, not Jesus. Popular opinion has conferred its titles and its sentence: Jesus will be crucified, and Barabbas saved.

Like words, sentences can roll off the tongue too, distorting meaning, obscuring truth, delivering unfounded though sometimes popular judgements. Lies flow, illusive words underpin conceits and deceits. What is truth anyway?

Through all this, the voice of Jesus still sings out, 'Everyone who belongs to the truth listens to my voice.' As we tumble through the verses of our discipleship, this surely is worth hanging on to. Jesus is the truth who will set us free.

Who do you say I am?

Prayer

Dear Jesus, the truth,
Make clean my soul from
All the dirt of sin.
I confess what seems
To be a constant
Grim tugging need for
Approval. The call
Of popular noise,
Opinion, action,
I struggle to sift
From your quiet voice.
Wash me inside out.
Rid me of the filth
That has stuck to me
And what I've chosen.
Especially the
Ideas, images
And ear worms that have
Become a truth that's
More vivid than you.
Kindly erase them.
Now, help me place in
My soul's sights and the
Source of my instincts
You. Truly king, whose
Cleansing saves the world
And even makes a
Case for me. Amen

7
Judgements
Good Friday 4

Then Pilate took Jesus and had him flogged. And the soldiers wove a crown of thorns and put it on his head, and they dressed him in a purple robe. They kept coming up to him, saying, 'Hail, King of the Jews!' and striking him on the face. Pilate went out again and said to them, 'Look, I am bringing him out to you to let you know that I find no case against him.' So Jesus came out, wearing the crown of thorns and the purple robe. Pilate said to them, 'Here is the man!' When the chief priests and the police saw him, they shouted, 'Crucify him! Crucify him!' Pilate said to them, 'Take him yourselves and crucify him; I find no case against him.' The Jews answered him, 'We have a law, and according to that law he ought to die because he has claimed to be the Son of God.' Now when Pilate heard this, he was more afraid than ever. He entered his headquarters again and asked Jesus, 'Where are you from?' But Jesus gave him no answer. Pilate therefore said to him, 'Do you refuse to speak to me? Do you not know that I have power to release you, and power to crucify you?' Jesus answered him, 'You would have no power over me unless it had been given you from above; therefore the one who handed me over to you is guilty of a greater sin.' From then on Pilate tried to release him, but the Jews cried out, 'If you release this man, you are no friend of the emperor. Everyone who claims to be a king sets himself against the emperor.' When Pilate heard these words, he brought Jesus outside and sat on the judge's bench at a place called The Stone Pavement, or in Hebrew Gabbatha. Now it was the day of Preparation for the Passover; and it was about noon. He said to the Jews, 'Here is your King!' They cried out, 'Away with him! Away with him! Crucify him!' Pilate asked them, 'Shall I crucify your King?' The chief priests answered, 'We have no king but the emperor.' Then he handed him over to them to be crucified.

(John 19.1–16)

Judgements

Where are you really from? Your parentage?
Who is your Father? Where's your home? What are
You doing here? Do you refuse to speak?
It's time to learn my language. Answer me.

You have no power over who may bridge
The great divide of death and reach the far
Off shore. Unless the strong gives to the weak.
Unless I am to you the breath to be.

Behold, here is your king, whose heritage
Is yours, he claims, is mine. As commissar
I neither cancel nor commend this freak.
I have no clarity of any plea.

It's written here that such a man should die.
The one good thing you'll do is crucify.

Reflection

When we are insecure about difference, or uncertain about our place in the scheme of things or want to display a little of what we perceive to be our own cultural superiority, then it is a cheap and easy option to play this out by making others feel that they are not at home. Where are you from? But where are you *really* from?

In our city streets and schools and offices and sometimes even palaces, questions such as these cut like knives through the mutual respect and friendship of our communities and reveal a nasty, reductive racism. Language, accent, appearance, religion, traditions of food, hair or clothing – all the things that tell of the rich variety of who we are and the families and communities that have birthed and shaped us – become ways of placing someone, presuming to know them without bothering to get to know them. They become ways of demonstrating power without offering the vulnerability involved in revealing ourselves and trying find common ground with another. They diminish both questioner and questioned.

Pilate's question to Jesus, 'Where are you from?' involves some similar assumptions, about religious belonging and standing, about cultural background and about perceived political allegiance. But it also goes much deeper, into the heart of who Jesus is. Where are you from? Who do you say you are? Pilate wants to know where Jesus has come from, who has sent him, and why he has come to the world.

Pilate fears that Jesus is trying to challenge the emperor for worldly power. Believing that he is challenging them, the religious authorities mock Jesus by calling him King of the Jews. And yet no evidence is found, and only empty arguments are presented. Under an uncomfortable spotlight, in a place between different interpretations, Pilate cannot reconcile these different anxieties and expectations. He is caught in the middle, a weak and vacillating leader, who fears for his own fragile grip on power and who mistrusts even himself. The answers to Pilate's questions bring their own judgement. Who do you say Jesus is? And who therefore am I?

Adam's poem captures the doubtful and insecure voice of Pilate. It's not only that Pilate cannot place Jesus culturally or in terms of his ancestry or geography, but also that he is not able get the measure of who Jesus really is. And so, his Pilate resorts to bullying with language: 'Do you refuse to speak? / It's time to learn my language. Answer me.'

There are Pilates in every community and in every congregation.

Jesus refuses to answer. He resists all the labels and will not play Pilate's language game. After all, questions are not really questions if we think we already know the answers and if we only ask them in order to bully and diminish our opponents.

So, Pilate resorts to a label laced with sarcasm; one that mocks and diminishes and condemns. 'Here is the man,' he proclaims, as the battered and beaten Jesus, clothed in purple and crowned with thorns, is paraded before the crowds. He means that Jesus is no man at all, and certainly no king, worldly or heavenly. But the judgement is turned on its head, because those who see the wounded and humiliated Jesus see both man and king. They see the love of God made manifest as God empties himself of power to become fully human. They see love that conquers evil, reaching across boundaries and borders to bring healing and salvation to people and nations.

Wherever we have come from, wherever we are travelling, whatever language we speak, whatever culture has shaped us, God knows who we really are. God comes to us in Jesus Christ, his identity in the world doubted and scorned, but his own understanding of his divine identity strong and clear. Since we are in him, our identity need never again be in question, to others or to ourselves. Even Pilate sees this: 'Behold, here is your king, whose heritage / Is yours, he claims, is mine.'

We do not find ourselves by drawing boundaries of culture, ethnicity or language around our identities. Neither barriers nor weapons, they are part of who we are. And whatever else we gloriously are, we are wholly in Christ.

We do not need to crucify each other to try to cancel out our own insecurity. The crucifixion ends those games of one-up-manship for ever. God has called time on the violence that is born of fear. We are all in Christ. The gift is ours to behold.

Who do you say I am?

Prayer

Jesus, the king and
Good Lord of glory,
I humbly beg you
Judge me according
To your faithfulness,
Your goodness and love.
Reach out across time
And space to find me.
You know who I am.
You created the
Rich variety
Of my being. The
Complexity is
No surprise to you.
You know me deeply.
Help me to judge well;
To know your power
Exercised in ways
Little understood;
To offer mercy
And, from your store of
Forgiveness, to be
One who gives to the
Broken world in the
Opposite spirit.
Here you are. I ask
You for the power
From above. Amen

8
Standing
Good Friday 5

So they took Jesus; and carrying the cross by himself, he went out to what is called The Place of the Skull, which in Hebrew is called Golgotha. There they crucified him, and with him two others, one on either side, with Jesus between them. Pilate also had an inscription written and put on the cross. It read, 'Jesus of Nazareth, the King of the Jews.' Many of the Jews read this inscription, because the place where Jesus was crucified was near the city; and it was written in Hebrew, in Latin and in Greek. Then the chief priests of the Jews said to Pilate, 'Do not write, "The King of the Jews", but, "This man said, I am King of the Jews."' Pilate answered, 'What I have written I have written.' When the soldiers had crucified Jesus, they took his clothes and divided them into four parts, one for each soldier. They also took his tunic; now the tunic was seamless, woven in one piece from the top. So they said to one another, 'Let us not tear it, but cast lots for it to see who will get it.' This was to fulfil what the scripture says, 'They divided my clothes among themselves, and for my clothing they cast lots.' And that is what the soldiers did. Meanwhile, standing near the cross of Jesus were his mother and his mother's sister, Mary the wife of Clopas, and Mary Magdalene. When Jesus saw his mother and the disciple whom he loved standing beside her, he said to his mother, 'Woman, here is your son.' Then he said to the disciple, 'Here is your mother.' And from that hour the disciple took her into his own home.

(John 19.16b–27)

Standing

With Mary, the one loved by Jesus stands
In silent daylight, a disciple still.
As naked violence held by pinioned hands
Is throttled by a glorious act of will.
The crucified one carries all the weight,
Absorbing it. Absorbing every thing
That otherwise can kill or damn our fate.
The static, vivid fight reads 'I am King'.
I argue for the part of him I want,
That quarter, or that cost or cross or crown
I'd rather not. Thank God! For through this font,
Baptized, we have the total debt paid down.
Imagining such freedom from my sin,
Adopted, loved, I move to take you in.

Reflection

When we see evil unfolding in front of us it is hard to know whether we should watch, so that suffering does not go unseen, unrecorded and unchallenged. Even when we lack power, there can be resistance in the level gaze of truth. Or we may choose to look away: from respect, out of desire not to be a voyeur, or to avoid being complicit. There is power too in restraint and refusal.

Those who watched and waited may not have been able to bear to cast their eyes on the body of their beloved Jesus. But they chose to stay and to stand with their Lord.

Adam's sonnet invites us to stay and to stand. Not standing by, in the sense of being a *by*-stander, letting things happen that we should have intervened in. Maybe not fully *under*-standing either; that will have to wait for eternity when the fullness of God's glory will be revealed. Instead, we are invited to stand now in prayerful solidarity, strong and fully present.

John does not describe much of Jesus' actual crucifixion, or his body on the cross. Whether or not he was able to watch, recounting may have been too much to bear. Instead, he tells us what this extraordinary event signifies, how it matters to those who are standing by, and what it means for the formation of a community of people who also stand in prayerful solidarity around the body of their crucified Saviour.

In Hebrew, in Latin, in Greek, John tells us, the presence of God in his Son is communicated to the whole world. Although his body is broken on the cross, Jesus of Nazareth is proclaimed as King of the world.

We have seen from different angles in John's Gospel who Jesus is, who other people say he is, and who they and we are as a result. We've seen Pilate play with meaning: 'So you are a King?' 'What is truth?' 'Here is the man!' Even now, almost at the point of Jesus' death, his significance is disputed. The chief priest doesn't want 'The King of the Jews' as an inscription on the cross, preferring the altogether more mocking, 'This man said, I am King of the Jews.'

Pilate stands his ground: 'What I have written, I have written.' I am never quite sure whether Pilate is dismissive because he is bored and wants to move on at this point, or whether his words point to an emerging recognition that Jesus was more than a political irritant. But this much is clear, the world will not easily understand who Jesus is, or what this means, and Pilate is no different.

Yet in the uncertainty of this moment of averted gazes, divided spoils and troubled consciences, something beautiful emerges. Before his death, Jesus focuses his own gaze on Mary, his mother, and John, his beloved disciple. And it is this gaze that creates the space for a new community to develop, as Mary and John reach out to create a new relationship, a new family, a new home: a household of faith. Behold!

As Mary and John turn to each other in impending grief, they also become united with Jesus in the love of the Father. Knowing that they have been adopted by God, they create the space for others too to be adopted, and to form a family, the church, which gathers and stands in prayerful witness and solidarity around the body and blood of their Saviour.

The poem lays out the options for what we might think we would want to keep of Jesus. Like the soldiers who crucify him, we could seek out a piece of Jesus: a 'quarter, or that cost or cross or crown'. These are no rewards, no spoils that we would wish to keep, but rather burdens that are too much for us to carry through life. It is only Jesus who can pay such a substantial price, only Jesus who can grasp the sin that binds us all, only Jesus who can free us from our debt.

Standing at the foot of the cross, the poem shows us moved not to grasp at spoils, but instead to receive a gift: 'Imagining such freedom from my sin, / Adopted, loved, I move to take you in.'

We are invited to receive love. To make room for the love of God in Jesus also to live in us. To believe even on this darkest of days that we belong in the light of Christ.

We can look beyond these scenes of the cross, which we too struggle to contemplate, because love can conquer our guilt and our fear. Loved and adopted by God, we can shift our own gaze beyond the broken body of Jesus on the cross and follow his loving gaze, as it generates a new community of hope.

This community today is us, God's Church. A household of faith, sharing wounds as well as joys, hurts as well as hope. Standing together.

Jesus' gaze of love invites each of us to join his family and to proclaim him as Lord and Saviour of the world.

Who do you say I am?

Prayer

Dear Jesus, hear me,
Lean down and listen
To this childlike cry.
I so desire to
Be in that number,
To be drawn further
Into your loving
Embrace, knowing my
True inheritance
With all the saints, how
Wide and long and high
And deep is your love.
To know this love that
Surpasses knowledge.
May I find my place
In your household, your
Communion table.
May the family
Likeness shine through me.
You focus your gaze
Upon me and I
Do the same to you,
Holding in my eye
The cost of the cross.
You write above me
A name spelled in love.
May your family
Ever grow. Amen

9
Given
Good Friday 6

After this, when Jesus knew that all was now finished, he said (in order to fulfil the scripture), 'I am thirsty.' A jar full of sour wine was standing there. So they put a sponge full of the wine on a branch of hyssop and held it to his mouth. When Jesus had received the wine, he said, 'It is finished.' Then he bowed his head and gave up his spirit. Since it was the day of Preparation, the Jews did not want the bodies left on the cross during the sabbath, especially because that sabbath was a day of great solemnity. So they asked Pilate to have the legs of the crucified men broken and the bodies removed. Then the soldiers came and broke the legs of the first and of the other who had been crucified with him. But when they came to Jesus and saw that he was already dead, they did not break his legs. Instead, one of the soldiers pierced his side with a spear, and at once blood and water came out. (He who saw this has testified so that you also may believe. His testimony is true, and he knows that he tells the truth.) These things occurred so that the scripture might be fulfilled, 'None of his bones shall be broken.' And again another passage of scripture says, 'They will look on the one whom they have pierced.' After these things, Joseph of Arimathea, who was a disciple of Jesus, though a secret one because of his fear of the Jews, asked Pilate to let him take away the body of Jesus. Pilate gave him permission; so he came and removed his body. Nicodemus, who had at first come to Jesus by night, also came, bringing a mixture of myrrh and aloes, weighing about a hundred pounds. They took the body of Jesus and wrapped it with the spices in linen cloths, according to the burial custom of the Jews. Now there was a garden in the place where he was crucified, and in the garden there was a new tomb in which no one had ever been laid. And so, because it was the Jewish day of Preparation, and the tomb was nearby, they laid Jesus there.

(John 19.28–42)

Given

A death-dark garden. Joseph came to take,
With Nicodemus, to a new-cut tomb.
Preparing for the final act they make
In pain, now finished, from a Christmas womb.
A sharp, long-promised piercing with a spear
Produced the liquid proof of love, in gall.
And though the theme of truth is hushed by fear
We witnesses cannot deny his call.
'I thirst.' It's done. No more to drink, the wine
To choking dregs consumed. Up on the wood
We see our saving, re-creation sign.
Now rest, my God, for it is very good.
The one who's loved and held shows 'I am he.'
Look through the night to day. 'You follow me.'

Reflection

The last time I walked home from a retreat, just past Salmon Lane Lock along London's Regent's Canal, I came across a man. Not a real *man*, but a *mannequin*, slumped in the undergrowth on the stone bank, legs sticking straight out towards the murky water. He was clothed in a candyfloss pink skirt, face a mess of smeared lipstick, a fixed, cosmetic gaze staring out from his shadowy branch cave. Over his shoulder, a down pipe spurted water from the flats above. Smells of the evening's lamb doner wafted from Commercial Road's takeaways, spices blending with woodsmoke from a nearby barge. Two geese floated serenely by.

In the stillness of a chapel, I might glimpse the peace that passes all understanding. I might draw near to God in bread and wine, being reminded that Jesus, the lamb of God, has taken away my sins and those of the whole world. In prayer, I might frame the needs of the people and communities that I love in the enduring love of God the Father, placing them within God's promise of salvation.

But in this place, on the darkling canal, in this beloved never-still city, peace, communion and hope are sometimes elusive. And if they are hard to find, how much harder are they to speak of. In a world of broken bodies and fragile identities, I struggle to find words to say who Jesus is. I want my life, my every footstep, my every breath, to dance and sing of the healing that takes away my hurts and insecurities, letting streams of sunlight into the dark corners of my soul; of the justice that rolls like a river through our communities, sweeping away islands of inequity and exclusion; and of the peace that reigns in me because Christ on the cross put an end forever to violence and retribution. But, like both Joseph of Arimathea and Nicodemus, my faith is often secret and shadowy, and my words few. I leave the guy in his waterside tomb and breathe in the evening's spices.

The first of Adam's Good Friday poems, 'Taken', captured the startling interruption of Judas, with soldiers and police from the chief priests and the Pharisees, entering the garden to arrest Jesus. In his final Good Friday poem, 'Given', we are in a different mood. There are some similarities in the poems. I notice especially the 'dread-dark' garden at the beginning of 'Taken', and the 'death-dark' garden now; as well as the insistent call in the last lines of both to follow Jesus. For me, the parallels underline what has shifted, and how far we have come with Jesus.

The story has been leading to this point, though it will lead us yet further. From the cradle of the Nativity, via the foretelling of Candlemas, referenced in Adam's poem in the 'Christmas womb' and the 'long-promised piercing', Jesus' life has been clothed in death as his death is now clothed in life. Although the darkness surrounds the light, the light is not overcome.

And it is not only that the overarching story lands here. The glimpses of kingdom life that we have watched Jesus reveal – captives released, sight recovered to the blind, and the oppressed set free – start to make sense in the light of Jesus' willing sacrifice on the cross, the gift of redemption for a sorrowful and broken world. It isn't yet fully realized. Jesus is still thirsty for justice and peace. But the kingdom is close by.

In his earlier encounter with Jesus, Nicodemus observed, 'We know that you are a teacher who has come from God; for no one can do these signs that you do apart from the presence of God' (John 3.2). As he carries Jesus' body to the garden tomb, Nicodemus surely sees the depth of truth in his own observation. The signs and miracles of Jesus are not just good deeds or encouraging moments; they point to a new economy of love, where the normal rules of debt and shame are undone, and where Jesus reveals to us God's abundant, generous and overwhelming love for humanity.

Given. This love is freely given. For every disciple of Christ, the task of working out how to live and speak of God is only just beginning. It is a lifelong calling to understand who Jesus is and to find words that begin to express the enormity of the love we know in him. Even John struggles to find the words, crossing back and forth between the Hebrew Scriptures, his present eyewitness knowledge, and the resurrection perspective of eternity.

But the good news is that although we are invited, no account is demanded of us. Coming from the heart of God, filled with both sorrow and love, Jesus has confronted the power of sin and death and has been victorious. Whether we sit grandly on a throne or broken at the canal side, we are redeemed. The gift has been given.

So, who do you say I am? Each of us is invited to join in with telling the story of God's love. What we have experienced cannot but change the stories of our lives: 'We witnesses cannot deny his call.' But even if we lack clarity, confidence and certainty, the story is told. We join in with its telling not out of duty or fear, but from love.

In the words of Adam's poem, 'The one who's loved and held shows "I am he." / Look through the night to day. "You follow me."'

Jesus shows us who he is, as he reveals that he has been sent from the very heart of God. As he is 'loved and held' by God, so too are we. And the one who is loved and held will lead God's beloved children into the light: from night to day, from death to life, from here into eternity.

Jesus, you are my Lord and God. This is who I say you are.

Prayer

Good Jesus who will
Forgive us our debts,
Take pity we ask
On all who are trapped
In darkness, trodden
Underfoot, grieving
Without end, at a
Loss, walking but with
No prospect of dawn.
Thank you that in your
New economy
There is the promise
Of blessing, of a
Justification
Which reverses the
Expectations of
Pain and hopelessness.
But now I simply
Ask you to wrap me,
Cover in your shroud
Those in the shadows.
Work a miracle.
Then, after that great
Battle, the silent
Victory becomes
Unlocked. May I and
All the world know that
New freedom. Amen

10
Giles
Holy Saturday 1

The tomb was nearby, they laid Jesus there.

(John 19.42b)

Giles

I want to whisper what the saints will sing
The cheer to triumph, celebration tune.
See scores of soldiers, angels wing by wing,
Lit not by sun, or sallow cast of moon.
I wonder, dearest, that this dream of place
Here home to stay in, to sustain and rest,
Is promise. Perfect. Our eternal space.
For life. For ever. Not as one more guest.
I sense the scene is set, the banquet laid,
The fighting done with, so a table spread.
Full field of wonder, which has all been paid
By him now seated, smiling, at the head.
'Dear friend, together let's take bread, drink wine.
Brave peace, beloved. Put your hand in mine.'

Reflection

Waiting is a kind of solidarity. When we wait, whether we are waiting for someone to die, or observing the rituals that come after their death, we are allowing ourselves to stay in a prayerfully patient space, neither clinging on, nor moving on too fast.

We may bring memories shaped as stories, captured as photographs or immortalized in snatches of song lyrics, the tracks of a misspent youth. Fragments, drawn together tentatively, anticipating a final verse.

Good Friday ended, the disciples prepared the nearby tomb and laid their brother Jesus inside it, a final act of accompaniment. I wonder how they looked back at the waiting they had endured with him, how they lived in the moment of Saturday's desolate uncertainty, and how they prepared their hearts for an as yet unknown future. Grief casts shadows in and from many directions, mingling anticipation, anguish and hope.

Adam writes of having accompanied his friend Giles so that he can see the 'table spread' and the 'full field of wonder' that are laid before him, with Jesus waiting to take his hand. There is gentle beauty in letting someone go and trusting that they are on the verge of being lit by a light that comes neither from the sun nor from the moon, but from God, our source of light and life. Friendship is celebrated as this vision is surveyed together. But only one person enters now into the promise of eternal rest.

For the one who remains, what remains? Is there guilt that we desired our loved one's suffering to end? It is not that we wanted them to go but, in our love, we may have known that leaving their bodily suffering behind would be both relief and release. Staying with the knowledge that we dangled for a while between hope and a desire for the end is hard. It is not disloyal, but it feels it.

There may also be curiosity, emptiness and searching. Where are they? Where have they gone? Many years ago, I experienced a partial molar pregnancy, a dangerous condition that can lead to a rare kind of cancer and always results in the death of the foetus. I had carried a dead baby for around five weeks before a scan showed the sad reality of non-viability. I felt betrayed – by my body, by my own hopes and anticipations, and by medical professionals: my symptoms had been disregarded and some test results ignored. Betrayal compounded the loneliness of loss.

Even in the preparation for surgery, I couldn't bear the thought of being separated from the baby I was still carrying. In the aftermath, I felt empty, as empty as a deserted tomb, but with, at that point, no glimpse of hope to sustain me.

My emptiness was not metaphysical; this loss was not only of expectation, but of flesh. As we drove away from the hospital after my surgery, I remember looking out across the bleak city and wondering where my baby was. As if I had carelessly mislaid him. *They have taken my beloved, and I do not know where they have laid him.*

In this limbo, is there still faith? Maybe. There is also unfaith: a state of longing for, but not quite being able to find God. This is the in-between time, when God is not absent, but when faith and hope are suspended. Whatever hope I might come to know, whatever faith might be restored to me, whatever light I might come to see, this moment is bleak and empty. I feel far from God, though I sense God at my shoulder.

The Gospels are silent. Words are obviously, painfully absent. There is no immediate comfort. As an oratorio of the heart, today has neither uplifting solos nor rousing choruses. Instead, it is a patient interlude, which picks up our life's melodies, weaving them back and forth in a new song of memory, whose patterns we cannot yet identify.

In time, there will be new stories, new feasts, new journeys. We will find ways to tell of who we have been together and who Jesus has been, and is, for us.

This Saturday, Jesus is never far away, but it is the notes of his absence that shape our song.

Prayer

Jesus, laid to rest,
We lay before you
The sins we repeat
And plead you to put
Them to death with you.
So now I wait, still.
I pause only to
Ask for patience to
Sit alone with you.

I do not know how
You will resolve the
Broken pieces of
Many tragedies
To make something more
Beautiful than was.
But I suspend my
Solutions and just
Leave them in the tomb.

It's hard, this waiting.
I want to know your
Comfort, but I can't
Even hear you breathe.
Still, my soul, be still.

This pause, this holy
Interlude is yours.
You take death itself
To the grave. I am
So grateful. Amen

II
Saturday
Holy Saturday 2

Early on the first day of the week, while it was still dark.

(John 20.1a)

Saturday

This Saturday, the day before the joy,
Lies empty as your body did of soul,
Of life and spirit. Contrast stark, your whole
Existence had been full up since a boy.
We laughed, shared friends and family. Delight
In storytelling, feasts and journeys made
To right some human wrongs. It seems you paid
In deeper pain, your passion crushed from fight.
Alive you saw me, knew me well, now spent.
Too late. I lack the power of that shout
Into the tomb of 'Lazarus, come out!'
Creating at your word the end you meant.
Yet my Redeemer lives. Where is thy sting
O death? On Sunday's dawn will rising bring.

Reflection

The cruellest hours are when the depths of night are about to become the dawn. Though faint hints of light on the horizon seem to offer hope, the weighted blanket of darkness is comfortably familiar. Moving on is harder than staying put.

It is early on the first day of the week, and still dark, when Mary Magdalene ventures to Jesus' tomb. I wonder if she is pained at this point that she can no longer cling on to the familiarity of Jesus, no longer summon up his face in her imagination. Perhaps remaining in darkness helps to keep those fading images alive for a little longer. Sunlight hurts the eyes, bleaching familiar recollections, crowding new people, landscapes and events into the precious vaults of dark memory. 'Storytelling, feasts and journeys' dissolve, and delight vanishes with them. We might prefer the darkness.

John's Gospel is on the cusp here: not just of night and day, or of life and death (and life again), but of meaning. As the dawn brightens, John's lens draws back, moving away from eyewitness account to begin to frame a drama of much greater significance. The story is no longer just what happened, but what those events meant – and will continue to mean, as they are told again, at daybreak, around charcoal fires, on shores across the world.

Who is Jesus for John? Who is Jesus for Mary Magdalene? Though the light may hurt their eyes, and darkness, a familiar friend, may tempt them back into comforting grief, both are somehow able to look forward, to discover the hope of the empty tomb, and to know that the risen Jesus is not only their saviour, but the saviour of the world.

It is not easy to carry on when the life of the one we loved has ended. It hurts even to be reminded that life continues, that day follows night, because to do so seems only to emphasize the death and darkness that we know and carry inside us still. Guilt may follow; why is it that life continues for me, but not for him?

Though our shouts do not have the power to bring the ones we have loved back to life again, life shuffles onwards. Though memories cannot be resurrected, relationships and bonds of friendship continue to develop; shared events are newly recollected, fresh rituals are formed, imagined conversations keep the flame of love alive. The company of saints is not a museum of fixed memorials, but an enlivening and generative reality that accompanies us, the whole company of believers, on our journey of faith. We walk together in the light.

It is painful to make this shift – from present to eternity, from material to spiritual, from individual to collective, and from darkness into light. Mary Magdalene begins to make it, as she steps out in darkness towards the empty tomb. John makes it as he opens a window from the life of Jesus on to the story of God's redeeming love.

And we may make it now too, even in grief, because we know the truth that Jesus was and is resurrected from the dead, and that eternal life is ours also.

Prayer

Dear Jesus, we're here.
Choosing not to hide
Ourselves from your look,
Waiting to be seen
When the blanket of
Darkness is lifted.
Saying to you that
We want that early
Light to dawn and turn
The next day into
The first day of life.
It's that hope and that
Expectation which
Means we wait here now.

I cannot hear, but feel
The company of
Saints and apostles
Wait with me for the
Glorious freedom
Promised. You mean for
All of us to live!

I offer up in
These wakeful moments
All those who are and
Have been on my heart.

I pray a joyful
Hush to fill my soul.

Jesus, come. Amen

12
Everything
Easter 1

Early on the first day of the week, while it was still dark, Mary Magdalene came to the tomb and saw that the stone had been removed from the tomb. So she ran and went to Simon Peter and the other disciple, the one whom Jesus loved, and said to them, 'They have taken the Lord out of the tomb, and we do not know where they have laid him.' Then Peter and the other disciple set out and went towards the tomb. The two were running together, but the other disciple outran Peter and reached the tomb first. He bent down to look in and saw the linen wrappings lying there, but he did not go in. Then Simon Peter came, following him, and went into the tomb. He saw the linen wrappings lying there, and the cloth that had been on Jesus' head, not lying with the linen wrappings but rolled up in a place by itself. Then the other disciple, who reached the tomb first, also went in, and he saw and believed; for as yet they did not understand the scripture, that he must rise from the dead. Then the disciples returned to their homes.

But Mary stood weeping outside the tomb. As she wept, she bent over to look into the tomb; and she saw two angels in white, sitting where the body of Jesus had been lying, one at the head and the other at the feet. They said to her, 'Woman, why are you weeping?' She said to them, 'They have taken away my Lord, and I do not know where they have laid him.' When she had said this, she turned round and saw Jesus standing there, but she did not know that it was Jesus. Jesus said to her, 'Woman, why are you weeping? For whom are you looking?' Supposing him to be the gardener, she said to him, 'Sir, if you have carried him away, tell me where you have laid him, and I will take him away.' Jesus said to her, 'Mary!' She turned and said to him in Hebrew, 'Rabbouni!' (which means Teacher). Jesus said to her, 'Do not hold on to me, because I have not yet ascended to the Father. But go to my brothers and say to them, "I am ascending to my Father and your Father, to my God and your God."' Mary Magdalene went and announced to the disciples, 'I have seen the Lord'; and she told them that he had said these things to her.

(John 20.1–18)

Everything

It's early. There's much more morning to break
On fear, commuting darkness to dispel
And here, even in this cathedral, make
Sweet love the legacy instead of hell.
But people underground have been set free!
Great light now comes to surface on the street.
We walk to work awake in unity
With love, transporting life in whom we meet.
At breakfast, at the meal which means I live
Without the need to fight another day,
He feeds me with a better word to give
Such love a-plenty. Go, in peace, his way.
The resurrection changes everything.
Behold: The coronation of our king.

Reflection

Can I let you in on a secret? Do you promise not to tell anyone?

I sing on the platforms and in the pedestrian tunnels of the London Underground. The acoustic is wonderful. I sound a far better singer than I really am. Tottenham Court Road tube station is my favourite – it has long, high, tiled passageways for passengers walking from the ticket hall to the trains. I also often sing on the platforms at Mile End, my local station. And a new discovery is the Elizabeth Line with its sleek escalators and nave-like hallways. It's like being inside the chamber of a guitar, with lots of noises reverberating and amplified, but with the melody finding its way to the top of the sound wave, taking me to the line that matters most.

I usually sing hymns, chants or worship songs. And sometimes, when I have a tickle in my feet, I dance. Not much, not even so you'd really notice if you walked past me, just a quick skip to the beat of the music of God's time.

I sing and dance in the morning – and the midday and the night, at rush hour and in times of quiet – but especially in the morning when the air is fresher and colder, and the notes seem to ring true.

The story of the resurrection has been told, sung and danced through centuries. Encountering the risen Jesus in the garden, early on the first day of the week, Mary Magdalene was the first witness to the resurrection. She named Jesus as 'Rabbouni!' (Teacher) and then ran to tell the disciples, 'I have seen the Lord.' How she reacted, who she said Jesus was, set the tone for we who have followed her.

Mary's response is first to worship – she turns herself towards Jesus and names him as her Teacher. And her second is to bear witness; she tells others the good news. Since those two actions, God has been praised and the good news has been passed on, from person to person, each telling another who Jesus is.

Because of that good news, we can worship together now. Jesus is our Lord and our God. This is who we say he is.

I appreciate the way that Adam's 'Everything' imagines all our churches as cathedrals in which the story of faith can reverberate. The story of the love of God in Jesus Christ is so enormous, so sacrificial and so abundant, that it liberates and saves the whole world: 'And here, even in this cathedral, make / Sweet love the legacy instead of hell. / But people underground have been set free!' We have been telling that story in our words and in our actions, here in cities, towns, suburbs and villages, for many centuries.

It is not only as if we have been underground on a daily commute and are coming up to the light to begin the new day. We are also underground when we bury or deny who Jesus is. There are people across the world who because they are per-secuted must live an underground faith and dare not speak or sing or dance the name of Jesus. But we are free: we walk in the light, and we can speak, sing and dance who Jesus is.

Because we know who Jesus is, we can also know more clearly who we are. As he tells Mary not to hold on to him, Jesus also tells her that he is 'ascending to my Father and your Father, to my God and your God.' We are children of God because Jesus is the Son of God. We are united with God because Jesus' sacrifice on the cross unites the earthly and the heavenly in one glorious act of love. This is who he is. This is who we are.

I appreciate the way that 'Everything' shows us living a resur-rection life. Adam's words help me connect what Jesus has done with how I now live. He writes, 'We walk to work awake in unity / With love, transporting life in whom we meet.'

I guess he's explaining why I feel a tune in the air and a spring in my step as I come up from the underground into the morning light. Jesus has united us forever through his death with the love of God. Nothing can separate us from that love. And so, as I cross Westminster Bridge with the sun coming up in the east, I can sing and dance the resurrection.

Jesus' identity doesn't depend on our saying who he is: God is God, Jesus is the Son of God, they are one, with the Holy Spirit. But we can name for good who Jesus is in all our cities, in our communities, in our families. We can live resurrection lives in the ways we love and serve others. We can point to the uniting love of God as we break down barriers between people and communities and see people as they truly are. We can choose to let ourselves be shaped by love so that others might see love by how we live. In Adam's words, 'He feeds me with a better word to give / Such love a-plenty.'

The first time I visited central London as a teenager was to perform in the Royal Festival Hall with a youth choir. Children of the 1980s, we used to sing a choral setting of a Barry Manilow song, 'One Voice'. The song begins with one voice in the darkness and builds up to a whole choir realizing that if each person sings what they truly believe, then they will be joined by more voices 'Singing in the darkness.'[1]

Of course, our setting was sung in the beginning with just one voice and then it built up as more voices joined in, creating harmonies and repetitions. I often return to that song as I pick out my melodies in the cathedrals of the transport system, as well as the bridges, the galleries, the parks and even the helipads of my now home city. It does take just one voice. First Mary Magdalene. Then the other women. Then the disciples. And the Gospel writers. And the early church. And now us. And people across the globe, even those whose cathedrals remain underground. So now there is indeed more than one voice, singing in the darkness. All proclaiming Jesus as Lord and Saviour.

This is no secret to keep, but a story to be shared. So, sing it at the bus stops, dance it in city squares, shout it from the bridges, proclaim it from the skyscrapers. And share it with the whole world. Who do you say I am? Jesus you are my Lord and Saviour.

---

1 Barry Manilow, One Voice © Universal Music Publishing Group.

Prayer

Forgiving Jesus,
With love, redeemer,
Speak absolution.
I receive your word
Which sets me free to
Worship you. Loosen
My tongue, my limbs, my
Imagination,
Running to you with
My whole person for
The resurrection
Changes everything!
Help me to witness
To that unity.
Not that I have to
But that I, like a
Bird, must simply sing.
New joy, rise up and
Overflow. Pour out
Your new wine, the most
Intoxicating
And potent vintage
To be stored in your
Cellars, where there is
More than enough for
All who are in need
Of life to the full.
Amen and Amen.

13
Chorus
Easter 2

When it was evening on that day, the first day of the week, and the doors of the house where the disciples had met were locked for fear of the Jews, Jesus came and stood among them and said, 'Peace be with you.' After he said this, he showed them his hands and his side. Then the disciples rejoiced when they saw the Lord. Jesus said to them again, 'Peace be with you. As the Father has sent me, so I send you.' When he had said this, he breathed on them and said to them, 'Receive the Holy Spirit. If you forgive the sins of any, they are forgiven them; if you retain the sins of any, they are retained.'

But Thomas (who was called the Twin), one of the twelve, was not with them when Jesus came. So the other disciples told him, 'We have seen the Lord.' But he said to them, 'Unless I see the mark of the nails in his hands, and put my finger in the mark of the nails and my hand in his side, I will not believe.'

A week later his disciples were again in the house, and Thomas was with them. Although the doors were shut, Jesus came and stood among them and said, 'Peace be with you.' Then he said to Thomas, 'Put your finger here and see my hands. Reach out your hand and put it in my side. Do not doubt but believe.' Thomas answered him, 'My Lord and my God!' Jesus said to him, 'Have you believed because you have seen me? Blessed are those who have not seen and yet have come to believe.'

Now Jesus did many other signs in the presence of his disciples, which are not written in this book. But these are written so that you may come to believe that Jesus is the Messiah, the Son of God, and that through believing you may have life in his name

(John 20.19–31)

Chorus

Awake, you new-born people! Rise up, rise!
Our universal suffrage is announced.
The first outburst is East, where evil's trounced.
As dark clears, hark! A chorus of surprise:
Weak barking in the creek becomes a song;
Tube tunnel tunes are soon a mighty swell;
Sprung forth, the wharf-entrapped canaries yell
For joy! A singing bishop skips along!
No daffs and eggs and bunnies serve to give
Away what's been a God-Almighty fight.
But new-washed streets shine crisp with dawn delight,
As now we know we've won: Our Jesus lives!
Sing free, dance fearless, friends. Shout loud the Creed:
   'Alleluia,
Christ is risen! He is risen indeed,
   Alleluia!'

Reflection

I love the elements of energy and surprise in Adam's poem, 'Chorus', as an outpouring of love, hope and liberation runs through the city, stirring up its inhabitants to join a chorus of joy. I recognize the particular form this takes in the area of East London where we live, with playful references to familiar creeks, tunnels, wharfs and roads. Perhaps you can imagine a similar Easter outpouring in your own landscape. There is singing and dancing, movement and life in streets that have been washed clean and now sparkle with potential.

In John's Gospel, as Jesus has returned to be with the disciples and others, gathering together as the household of faith, he breathes new life into them. 'Receive the Holy Spirit,' he says, before reminding them of their responsibility to bring peace and forgiveness to a fractured world.

Those who are gathered – and Thomas, who fears he has missed out, but whose hand is drawn later into the wounded side of Jesus – are not only stirred up, enlivened and energized by the breath of God within them, like the dry bones in Ezekiel 37.9. They are also sent out, with a stupendous, world-changing instruction to bring peace to households and communities. This is not just any sending out: this is being sent out in the power of the Holy Spirit, and with the authority of the one who was himself sent from God: 'As the Father has sent me, so I send you.'

The peace that they will bring stems from this Sunday evening gathering of the faithful. It is rooted in worship, sharing the body and blood of Jesus, and is shaped by a physical encounter with him. It is real, and it can cope with reality, including fear and doubt: the bloodied hands of Thomas bear witness to the place of human insecurity and uncertainty within faith. Because it is breathed from the Spirit of God, it has power to shape whole communities and to offer fullness of life for all.

At its heart, this peace comes from knowing Jesus, from recognizing who he is. It comes from the security of faith. It comes from being able, with Thomas, to proclaim Jesus as 'My Lord and my God!' And although the context may change, from Jerusalem to London, across continents and islands, we too can proclaim Jesus as our Lord and our God; we too can be bearers of his peace.

Breathing life into Jesus as the Word made flesh, John shows us both how to read and to live the Gospel. How to read it; because, unlike Pilate and Herod, John knows the value of meanings, judgements and commitments. 'What I have written, I have written' only counts for something if what is written is good and true. John's words point us to God, the source of all goodness and truth. How to live it; because the actions of John's Jesus are consonant with who he says he is, an outpouring of God's love expressed through loving service and sacrifice. We are invited to live not only in ways that are similarly loving, but in ways that reveal the congruity of our actions and our identity: like seaside rock, L-O-V-E is to run through our core.

In church communities, I keep being surprised by God's Spirit breathed among us. When the story of God is kept alive, in prayer, teaching, song and dance, people are stirred up to ordinary and extraordinary acts of love, witness and service. When faith is shared in ways that are real and authentic, then new believers encounter God, and they in turn are sent out as disciples on to our city streets, finding fresh ways of calling people back to the love of God.

This is how we speak of Jesus. This is how our lives speak of Jesus. This is how we reflect who we say he is. This is Jesus, our Lord, and our God.

As words of joy swell through the underground tubes of the organ that is our city, and as 'new-washed streets shine crisp with dawn delight', sound and light combine into a loud and fearless Creed: 'Alleluia, / Christ is risen! / He is risen indeed.'

With the peace of the resurrected Jesus Christ in our hearts, let us sing, dance and skip this story of God's love.

Prayer

Risen Jesus, the
Innocent captive,
Who did not fight back
But bears the marks of
Love on your body
Even to this day.
Breathe on me the peace
Which the world cannot
Give nor understands.
Commission me as
A peacemaker, with
Wisdom sufficient
For each occasion.
I ask you to stand
With me, among the
Conflicts and chasms
That separate us.
The challenges you
Call me into are
Ones you already
Know how to resolve.
I believe you are
Not just who I need
But that nobody
May miss out the peace
Which only you bring.
I believe and I
Worship you. Amen

14
Fishtails
Easter 3

After these things Jesus showed himself again to the disciples by the Sea of Tiberias; and he showed himself in this way. Gathered there together were Simon Peter, Thomas called the Twin, Nathanael of Cana in Galilee, the sons of Zebedee, and two others of his disciples. Simon Peter said to them, 'I am going fishing.' They said to him, 'We will go with you.' They went out and got into the boat, but that night they caught nothing.

Just after daybreak, Jesus stood on the beach; but the disciples did not know that it was Jesus. Jesus said to them, 'Children, you have no fish, have you?' They answered him, 'No.' He said to them, 'Cast the net to the right side of the boat, and you will find some.' So they cast it, and now they were not able to haul it in because there were so many fish. That disciple whom Jesus loved said to Peter, 'It is the Lord!' When Simon Peter heard that it was the Lord, he put on some clothes, for he was naked, and jumped into the lake. But the other disciples came in the boat, dragging the net full of fish, for they were not far from the land, only about a hundred yards off.

When they had gone ashore, they saw a charcoal fire there, with fish on it, and bread. Jesus said to them, 'Bring some of the fish that you have just caught.' So Simon Peter went aboard and hauled the net ashore, full of large fish, a hundred and fifty-three of them; and though there were so many, the net was not torn. Jesus said to them, 'Come and have breakfast.' Now none of the disciples dared to ask him, 'Who are you?' because they knew it was the Lord. Jesus came and took the bread and gave it to them, and did the same with the fish. This was now the third time that Jesus appeared to the disciples after he was raised from the dead.

When they had finished breakfast, Jesus said to Simon Peter, 'Simon son of John, do you love me more than these?' He said to him, 'Yes, Lord; you know that I love you.' Jesus said to him, 'Feed my lambs.' A second time he said to him, 'Simon son of John, do you love me?' He said to him, 'Yes, Lord; you know that I love you.' Jesus said to him, 'Tend my sheep.' He said to him the third time, 'Simon son of John, do you love me?'

Peter felt hurt because he said to him the third time, 'Do you love me?' And he said to him, 'Lord, you know everything; you know that I love you.' Jesus said to him, 'Feed my sheep. Very truly, I tell you, when you were younger, you used to fasten your own belt and to go wherever you wished. But when you grow old, you will stretch out your hands, and someone else will fasten a belt around you and take you where you do not wish to go.' (He said this to indicate the kind of death by which he would glorify God.) After this he said to him, 'Follow me.'

Peter turned and saw the disciple whom Jesus loved following them; he was the one who had reclined next to Jesus at the supper and had said, 'Lord, who is it that is going to betray you?' When Peter saw him, he said to Jesus, 'Lord, what about him?' Jesus said to him, 'If it is my will that he remain until I come, what is that to you? Follow me!' So the rumour spread in the community that this disciple would not die. Yet Jesus did not say to him that he would not die, but, 'If it is my will that he remain until I come, what is that to you?'

This is the disciple who is testifying to these things and has written them, and we know that his testimony is true. But there are also many other things that Jesus did; if every one of them were written down, I suppose that the world itself could not contain the books that would be written.

(John 21.1–25)

Fishtails

I haven't brought in anything to eat.
My contribution's meagre, if at all.
I feel a certain failure, or a cheat.
The portion I should get will be quite small.
The task that I was given is a mess.
It's two steps forward, one great leap right back.
The only payment coming is the stress
Of finding that I'm heading for the sack.
He calls me over: 'Sit here, have some food.
That explanation's for another day.
Good news, look see our partnership's accrued
Outstanding winnings. Thanks. What can I say?'
My fishtail fortune! No one's out of reach
With Jesus. Come, have breakfast on the beach.

Reflection

It is early in the morning, and I can smell the charcoal on the air, see crumbs falling on the beach as bread is broken to share, and wet fish prepared on the stones. At the side of the boat, many more fish have been hauled ashore, an abundant catch, and yet the fishing net has not torn. It has held together. And there is Jesus, inviting me in: 'Come and have breakfast.'

I wonder how I am feeling. I've been through so much with Jesus, listened to his teaching, seen his miracles, watched the crowds follow and a close band of disciples gather around him: living, learning, loving. I've seen him arrested, tried, tortured and put to death on a cross. I've seen his empty tomb and known that he has risen from the dead. And now I'm trying to work out what happens next. Who do I say Jesus is? Who?

When I saw him from the boat, on the beach, I felt quite despondent. We all knew we were meant to be fishing. Jesus had told us that we were to fish for people. But however often we put the nets over the side, just as we'd always done, we never caught anything.

I thought we'd be travelling the world, sharing the hope of the resurrection with all the nations. I thought I'd know how to live this new life that he promised ... and gave. But then there I was, back out on the old boat, business as usual, but actually worse than usual, because those darned fish didn't want to come anywhere near our nets.

And there was Jesus standing on the shore, saying, 'Children, you have no fish, have you?'

His question felt sharp and kind at the same time. I suppose if we keep doing the same old things, we're going to get the same catch. So, we switched sides, and suddenly the nets were teeming with large, wriggling, shining, scaly fish, all kinds. A hundred and fifty-three, to be precise.

Simon Peter, always the one for a rash gesture, jumped in. First, he swam to shore, to Jesus, of course, and then he came back aboard to draw the heavy nets in. As Jesus prepares the breakfast, I can see that Peter is so very keen. And I know why. The last time he stood around a charcoal fire, when Jesus had just been arrested, Peter denied him. Three times he insisted he didn't know who Jesus was. And the cock crowed. And Jesus was taken off to be tried before Pilate.

Here we are now, fish smoking on the coals. Jesus is with us and inviting us to be with him again, to eat with him, to lean in close and breathe in his presence, to know peace in him, even when the world is all at odds. We don't just settle into our old ways, though. We can hear Jesus offering to Peter love, forgiveness and trust even after the damage of his betrayal. We can see Peter standing tall again, beginning to know what forgiveness feels like. We can feel ourselves being shaped too, formed in the pattern of love, recreated to love and care for each other. Perhaps we are becoming a little more like Jesus.

As he speaks, it seems clearer not only who he is, but also who we are. We're learning who we will say Jesus is, even when he's not here, no longer right before our eyes.

Three times Peter calls Jesus 'Lord!' Three times Jesus tells Peter how to show he loves him. 'Feed my lambs,' he says. 'Tend my sheep.' 'Feed my sheep.'

I'm no shepherd, but even I know what he means. We're to care for the new followers, the young ones, those who need to draw close and find the milk that gives them life and helps them grow. We're to see off the threats, from outside and in, teaching, guiding, rebuking, keeping one another well in the fold. And we're to feed each other, sitting around charcoal fires on shores the world over, with people from north and south and east and west, feasting on the memory of Jesus, tasting justice and peace.

When I saw him standing on the shore, I knew it was him. Not in the sense of *actually* seeing him. I couldn't. It was too far. I knew it was him because I felt it in my guts. I feel it again now, with him here round the fire with us, and I trust I will feel it even when he's gone. Knowing Jesus means being stirred up to care for others. This is who I am now because this is who I know he is. Knowing Jesus means yearning to follow his way, live his teaching, and make that real whether I'm at work on the lake or sharing the good news around the world. Knowing Jesus means peace: abiding in him, resting in his arms, feeling the beating of his heart, and through him, the very heart of God.

He's not going to keep coming back, at least not like this. And there will be others who will never have met him, who have never seen him first hand. But somehow, we will keep lighting charcoal fires, keep sitting and eating together, caring for each other, breathing in his presence as the smoke settles in our hair, telling together the stories of his love.

I understand now why Thomas was so keen to put his hands in Jesus' side to touch, to prove, to know that it was really Jesus standing in front of him. But Jesus said that the ones who are truly blessed are the ones who haven't seen yet who have still believed. Don't get me wrong: I'd probably have done what Thomas did. I'd have wanted some proof.

But how are others – every Galilean, every Roman, every Greek, all those who will never have met Jesus – how are they going to know Jesus if they haven't ever touched him?

Thomas knew who Jesus was. And he found the words to say it: 'My Lord and my God!'

I can find those words. I believe in Jesus, my Lord and my God. I know who Jesus is, even when he's far off on the shore. I know him now as we gather, forgiven, loved and free. As we eat together and remember how he was with us. And I will know him again, each time we break bread together.

There will be others, who have not seen Jesus, who also believe. Round charcoal fires, they will know, deep in their guts, that Jesus is present with them. They will find the words to tell the stories and to share the good news of the one who greets them from the shore, who tends and feeds them and who loves them into eternity.

And you. Do you know Jesus too? Who do you say he is?

Prayer

Jesus, who was so
Falsely accused and
Sentenced for sinners
Whom I have let down
Time and time again,
Each morning there is
A fresh start with you.
'Come and have breakfast.'
You beckon me to
Sit alongside you
So I do that now.

There are many tasks.
I'm not sure what will
Happen next, so first
You feed me, then you
Call me to follow.
What are you serving
Me today, my friend?
What word or morning
Revelation do
You have to chew on?

I digest your love,
Offered warm from the
Fire of forgiveness.
I know you. Now you
Let me know you more.
I say you are my
Lord, my God. Amen

Coda

So, who do you say that I am? We met
Before, not so? Through friends who were so kind,
Some years ago, I'd almost place a bet.
It doesn't really matter, never mind.
But who do you say that I am? From time
To time I've listened, heard the story told
And thought there might be something that's sublime,
A spirit or a presence very old.
No, who do you say that I am? I long
For light to lift the veil, pierce through the mist,
Forget the past, give purpose, to belong,
Find out the route, for truth to speak, exist.
I am your friend, your ancient way, your call.
You are! My Lord, my God. Be thou my all.